VOLUME CONTROL

a guidebook for highly sensitive people in a

loud & spiky world

Written & doodled by Jen Butler

The author of Volume Control is not a physician. The ideas and suggestions in this book are not intended to replace the medical advice of trained professionals.

This book mentions the topic of suicidality, depression, and addiction, based on the author's personal experience. If you or a loved one are struggling, the following resources are available to help 24/7:

Suicide Hotline Chat — https://988lifeline.org/chat/
Suicide Hotline — Call or text 988 (U.S. only)

We share more resources in the **Resources** section at the end of the book. **You don't have to suffer alone, precious human.**

@JENBUTLERSAYS

I wrote this book for myself, to help me learn to navigate this loud and spiky human experience. So, I dedicate this book to you, younger Jen. Thank you for not giving up.

If you feel alone, out of place, or struggle with being human...

This guidebook is for you.

Volume turned up on life (intro)

The human experience is a heavy lift. Can we get real about that for a moment? I understand that being alive is a miracle – I truly do – but it's a messy, terrifying, unscripted, wiggly-worm, shitshow of a miracle.

We need more of that wiggly-worm realness. Otherwise, we compare our messy behind-the-scenes to other people's highlight reels.

We shame and ostracize ourselves because our panicky, wiggly insides look nothing like *their* filtered smiles with perfectly placed freckles. Rather than bullying ourselves for the mess, *let's own it.*

I'm not talking about wallowing or trauma bonding here. I'm talking about connecting from a rigorously honest place. By owning and accepting the fact that being a human *is really freaking hard*, we can then go: Okay. True. **So, now what?**

How can we learn to engage with life *right now*, rather than hiding and keeping ourselves stuck?

That's what *Volume Control* is all about.

A quick note about VOLUME CONTROL: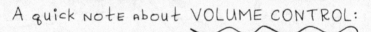

IN this book, VOLUME REFERS to the PERCEIVED loudNESS OR intensity of an EXPERIENCE. This could bE a sound, a sight, a human interaction, or an emotional reaction.

CONTROL REFERS to the powER to manage, direct, regulate, or command one's internal EXPERIENCE.

So, when I say VOLUME CONTROL, I mean: The power to internally regulate one's perception of the loudness or intensity of life.

WE may not bE able to control how loud OR intense the external world is, but wE CAN leARN to control our perception of and reaction to it.

Before we delve into emotional regulation tricks — or the story of my very public fight with a grocery store self-checkout machine — let's look at some of what we juggle as humans.

We have smooshy flesh vehicles that produce odor and sprout hairs[1] in inconvenient places. There are forces like gravity and time, which combine efforts to slowly morph us into melted birthday candles. We must feed ourselves and other living beings, *multiple times a day*. Jobs. Money. Bills. Exercise. Hygiene. Relationships. Keeping the Duolingo owl happy. Not to mention the heavier lifts like illness, inequality, trauma, and walking face-first into spiderwebs. And yet, it seems like the only widely acceptable response to the human experience is to spew gratitude from every available orifice.

---

[1] Some hair is encouraged or even glorified; most is not.

But wait, there's more! On top of all that, there are these finicky things called feelings. And for some of us, the volume is turned up *really high* on those feelings.

Life is loud for me. It always has been. Externally, lights are bright, sounds are overwhelming (mouth noises are the worst), and clothes are constricting. My skin feels too tight sometimes, my bones too pointy. Even the necessity for air can feel claustrophobic. Internally, emotions and thoughts become so intense that my cells feel like angry ants desperate to dance right out of my body.

And no matter which emotional state I find myself in, the volume knob defaults to **MAX**, as in *maximum volume.*

Other people's reactions and words feel "loud," too. Basic human things – like rejection or a stranger's scowl – can hijack my nervous system and elicit a giant emotional response that is wholly out of proportion to the tiny thing happening.

I don't dip my toes into each emotional state; *I do an epically awkward swan dive and become fully immersed.* I don't get a little sad; *I feel like I'm sinking in the Quicksand of Despair,* certain that life has always been and will always be this miserable.

There are other times when my emotional state flings to the other end of the extreme. I'll hear a bird sing and be overcome by how amazing birds are. How they weave their little nests and barf up half-eaten worms to their babies. I'll feel awe and appreciation bursting from my cells like little rainbow fireworks of glee.

And then, I'll just start weeping.

At the beauty of bird barf.

I was initially ashamed of my hypersensitivity, deeply and gutturally overwhelmed by the simple act of being alive. I was rarely fully present in my body because each moment was sensory overload and *too much* to handle. It felt like my soul was flipped upside down and flailing around above my head like a wacky waving inflatable arm-flailing tube man, rather than being embodied in my flesh.

I was either in my body and fending off panic attacks, or I was floating outside of my body and *feeling nothing*. That all-or-nothing dissonance made me feel crazy and detached, like I was multiple scattered bits rather than a whole human.

I'd see other people who seemed to be having a blast on this human ride, like they received some guidebook that Amazon forgot to deliver to me[2]. Meanwhile, my emotional and energetic microphones were so sensitive, I was picking up on sounds and vibes and nuances that my nervous system simply wasn't equipped to handle. Every day, I felt like my body and mind were under attack. I was overstimulated and exhausted in my cells, in my soul. From this existential exhaustion emerged alarms in my head that would repeatedly screech the lie that *I was a burden, and death was the only way out.*

A quick note: I do openly share about my experience with suicidality in this book. And really, it's not so much that I wanted to die — *I wanted to cease existence.* Poof! Gone without a trace, without a mess for anyone to find or clean up, and without heartbreak for my family. Sometimes, I admittedly still romanticize the thought of disappearing[3].

---

[2] No issue delivering the inflatable dinosaur or 12-pack of enemas, though. Odd priorities, Amazon.

[3] Except now I romanticize about disappearing to the woods and becoming a bog witch.

Good news: The lessons, tips, and tricks in this guidebook can help anyone who struggles with emotional regulation. If you're not plagued by a deep yearning to die (Yay!), replace any mention of suicidality with whatever you use to numb your feelings. Suicidality, for me, was another expression of what others may experience as alcohol or drug abuse, gambling, overeating or undereating, or any other behavior we use to avoid our big, uncomfortable feelings.

For a long time, I thought the loudness — the intensity with which I felt everything — meant there was something wrong with me. I felt panicky and awkward and alone. I went to multiple doctors, desperate for an "answer," and received contradicting diagnoses from each. Finally, I begrudgingly considered that maybe I needed to look *inside* rather than outside for guidance.

So, **I got curious**. I volunteered as tribute to be the subject of my own research project. I started small by simply asking myself questions.

Was I all of the diagnoses, some of them, or none of them? Was I like this because of nature, or nurture, or both? Was I merely a big, tangled knot of trauma responses? Would life always be this way? Could someone like me even handle the big, lofty dreams I'd always had? Or was I doomed to forever hide under a weighted blanket in a dim room, taking deep breaths in an effort to fend off daily panic attacks? Most of all: *Was I the only one who experienced life like this?*

Through my content creation (*@jenbutlersays*) and candidly sharing my journey with the world, I'm learning that I'm not alone in my experience. (Hooray for me not being alone!) ... (Boo for other people struggling with being human!) I've learned that, for some of us, life is extra loud and disorienting. The basic day-to-day may not come easily to us. Some days, it feels downright debilitating.

This book is in your hands as evidence that you are not alone, and that we can learn to cope, regulate, and live a full life as highly sensitive people. Also, to help make the content even more palatable, there are cute doodles and illustrations.

A picture book?! *Praise the Goddess of Bird Barf.*

Let's do an epically awkward swan dive into *Volume Control* **together**, shall we?

TOC: the basics

TOC: choose your own adventure

*Choose your emotional regulation adventure based on where your current emotional state lands on this **1-10** "scale".*

(More details on the next pages.)

Emotional state	Description	Page
1 MELTDOWN	**Read when:** • Everything is the worst. • Nothing seems worth it. • You're sobbing on the floor. • You feel like you're going to implode or explode. *(Add your own.)* • • •	*41*
2 BARELY HANGING ON	**Read when:** • Sensitivities are high. • People are super annoying. • You feel inferior to others. • Life feels gray and dull. *(Add your own.)* • • •	*71*
3 THE FUCK-ITS	**Read when:** • You start judging people. • You have a poopy attitude. • You *just don't wanna.* • You're angry at whoever signed you up for this. *(Add your own.)* • • •	*101*

Emotional state	Description	Page
7 THE SUN IS SHINING	**Read when:** • You've realized: *Oh wait. Life isn't so bad.* • You hear the birds again! • A **1-4** seems silly now. • Energy and clarity are returning. *(Add your own.)* • • •	*215*
8-10 IN THE GROOVE	**Read when:** • Life is going well. • Synchronicities abound. • You feel in alignment, clear on next steps. • You're (*gulp!*) excited. *(Add your own.)* • • •	*235*
11 KING OF THE WORLD	**Read when:** • Your ego is GIANT. • You feel superior to others. • You're freaking AMPED. • You're craving a drastic leap of faith with zero plan. *(Add your own.)* • • •	*255*

The blobs (who this book is for)

I'm sharing this book for two groups[4] of people:

- **Blob (group) 1: The Sensitive** – These are the folks who have the volume turned up on life. They hopefully recognize that they can't control how loud or intense the external world is, and they want to learn how to control their perception of and reaction to life.

- **Blob (group) +1: The Supporter** – These are the cheerleaders, the stubbornly loyal people whose loved one is highly sensitive and struggles with emotional regulation.

Blob 1 – The Sensitive: If you have the volume turned up on life, you likely know it. You may be someone who hides, cries a lot, numbs, cares too much, gets debilitated by fear, or swears they're feeling someone else's feelings. Maybe you hear voices or can sense animals or

---

[4] When presenting this book idea in a live, recorded meeting, I forgot the word "group" and instead said "two blobs of people." No one batted an eye or corrected me. Thus, the *blobs* were born.

nature. Perhaps you have mind-blowing highs and debilitating lows, or a slew of diagnoses. If you're anything like me, you may feel crazy or have to work extra hard to stay on Earth each day because *this just doesn't feel like home.*

Blob +1 – The Supporter: If you love someone who is highly sensitive and struggling, you may feel helpless, hopeless, and exhausted (understandably so). Or, maybe you need a behind-the-scenes view into how that person operates so you can shift out of "fixing" and into *supporting.*

There's also the lucky blend of someone who's a Sensitive *and* a Supporter, which may look something like this:

Whatever your specific situation is: you're not crazy, and you're not alone. I really, truly mean that from the bottom of my toes, which are currently in mismatched monster socks.

I'm not a doctor, and I don't know your individual battle. I won't talk to you from a place of being higher up than you, because I'm not. I still have the volume turned up on life. I'm still not the biggest fan of being human (though I am becoming leery friends with the human experience). I've spent most of my life sharing bunk beds with suicidality, addiction, codependency, disordered eating, and a general disdain for existence. I've numbed myself, tried to kill myself, failed, and ultimately realized: *Well, I guess I ought to learn to live.*

When I was in my deepest, darkest depression and felt like my sensitivities were a curse, I wish someone would have been real with me about their own experience so that I didn't feel so alone in mine.

Most books I found were prescriptive ones, written by people who claimed to have answers but spoke from outside the realm of actual lived experience. That really didn't cut it for me. So, I wrote my own darn book to help bridge the communication gap between my low lows and high highs.

And, after many years of testing this guidebook out on myself, I'm sharing it with you.

To me from me (the making of this book)

Through the whiplash of feeling like a rag doll flung from different emotional states, I started keeping track of what I felt. When struggling, I wrote down what I needed from Future Jen. When in a more grounded, less reactive place, I'd read and respond. When inevitably struggling again, I'd go back and reference the ongoing dialogue between those Past Jens. My words anchored me into reality faster and faster each time I read them.

I realize now that I was bridging the communication gap between my different aspects of self.

Whereas all emotions initially felt like "AAAHHHH!"... this process of self-inquiry helped me get in tune with my different emotions, no matter how intense they felt. I learned that a handful of them were more prominent and common.

Committing to the "volume control" analogy, let's say that each emotional state is a channel preset on a radio, where it may look like this:

radio channels 1 – 10

In short, the emotional presets are: **1** (Meltdown), **2** (Barely hanging on), **3** (The fuck-its), **4** (Something's not right), **5** (Robot mode), **6** (Cautiously content), **7** (The sun is shining), and **8-10** (In the groove).

I've also added two that are off the charts for those who have high highs and tend toward burnout: **11** (King of the world), and **0** (Burnout).

While this **1-10** setup may seem like a **1** is *bad* and a **10** is *good*, I've found that *every emotion can be equally uncomfortable*. Music can be uncomfortably loud whether it's death metal, classical, or Alanis Morissette. Same goes for these emotional radio presets. I'm just as likely to blow up my life in a MAXed out **1** headspace as I am a MAXed out **11**, or a MAXed out **5**. When life is loud, *it's loud*.

I built a table of contents with these emotional presets alongside doodles of what I thought the feelings *looked* like. That way, when I'm feeling a certain kind of way and need support for that specific mindset, I can quickly find its corresponding section. Plus, there's room for you to customize the TOC (table of contents) so that you can more quickly find the support you need.

(You'll see a bonus section at the end of the book called **+1**, for Supporters. I wrote that part with help from my friends and family, who graciously support me and other folks with volume control struggles.)

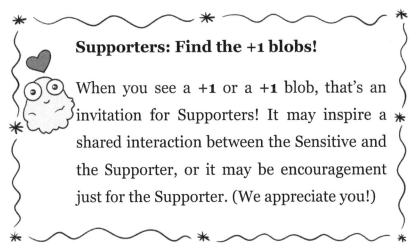

Supporters: Find the +1 blobs!

When you see a **+1** or a **+1** blob, that's an invitation for Supporters! It may inspire a shared interaction between the Sensitive and the Supporter, or it may be encouragement just for the Supporter. (We appreciate you!)

I've used this guidebook for years now to help me keep moving forward even when life feels extra loud and spiky. I'm still a work in progress. I must check in with myself regularly, and I do a lot of maintenance work to stay on Earth. My daily life consists of little course corrections (most of which are in this book) to snap out of panic and settle back into reality, into my body. Over the course of the last decade, I've been retraining my brain, rewriting my internal narratives, and helping my sweet nervous system relearn what is and is not a threat. Like potty training a puppy, I've needed patience and repetition. And a sense of humor[5].

I'm still learning how to fine-tune my volume control so that I can maintain my beautiful hypersensitivity and engage with, y'know, *real life*. I want to feel things deeply,

---

[5] Because what else can I do but laugh when my 5-month-old puppy, Daisy, poops IN THE AIR VENT?!

but I want to do so without sinking too deep or flying too high. I want to experience life, not hide from it.

For me, *it's not about trying to make life quieter.* I spent decades expecting everyone else to adjust how they lived in order to avoid triggering me, but that's not sustainable or fair. **I needed to address what it was within me that I was afraid to trigger.** Work through it, heal it, rewrite it. I needed to learn to feel safe in my body and regulate my own emotional reactions so I could respond like an adult instead of a three-year-old who didn't get the Squishmallow they wanted.

It's exhausting work at times. The tips and tricks in this book took me many years and countless tears to compile. I believe our sensitivities and the depth with which we experience life gives us the power to effect positive change. I think we're kind of like superheroes in the making. Adorably quirky, easily overwhelmed superheroes.

If you're sitting in fart pajamas[6], haven't showered in 11 days, and feel like you have sweaters on your teeth due to lack of teeth-brushing, effecting positive change may seem like a laughable concept. When I was in the darkest depths of suicidality, I kept seeing these visuals in my mind of me writing books and movies, speaking onstage, and helping others like me. This made me want to crawl deeper into my hole of darkness *because I seemed so impossibly far away from that other reality*. There was "no way" I'd be able to handle the potential rejection of an audience of people; I couldn't even leave my house without a panic attack!

And yet, here I am. Doing the scary, exciting things *without wanting to die afterward*. Living the life I saw in my mind. And then openly sharing about it online. *Wild.*

This manual consists of the important lessons I've learned — and sometimes forget — in a way that's easy for me to navigate when I'm in rough places, and important for me to reference when I'm teetering on feeling *too* good. That's why I went with the choose-your-own-adventure vibe. You can read *Volume Control* from beginning to end, and/or you can adventure to whichever section matches your current emotional state.

---

[6] Fart pajamas are the jammies we wear multiple days in a row where the stank becomes embedded in the threads. *If you know, you know.*

This book's course corrections are like bumpers in bowling, helping me to move forward on my journey rather than getting caught in the gutter. I use it as a cheat sheet, really. When I feel lost or frazzled and need a reminder of how to best handle my current state, I reference these pages.

You know the movie (and novel) *The Notebook?* Spoiler alert if you don't: the "notebook" in the story was written by a woman with Alzheimer's, intended to be read to her whenever she forgot who she was. *Volume Control* is my Notebook[7] to myself. *Super romantic, right?*

A note on the language I use throughout this book: I prefer conversational analogies and playful phrases over medical language. For example, rather than calling something a depressive episode, I may say I'm: in the Suck; in the Ouch; on the Struggle Bus; in the Quicksand; in a Valley; in a Brain Storm... and so on. These phrases and words are more resonant to me, and I hope they are for you.

---

[7] Except minus Alzheimer's and Ryan Gosling. You win some, you lose some.

Find what works (tips for reading)

Self-tolerance

The *Volume Control* tips and tricks cover topics such as self-compassion, honesty, acceptance, and so on. Some of what I recommend may feel overwhelming or even impossible.

That's totally okay, and totally normal.

I've been on this recovery journey for 10+ years, and I'm still trying to learn how to be nice to myself, to give myself even a sliver of the care, forgiveness, and patience that I offer others.

I remember when I first learned about the concept of self-love. I was like: "Um. That's cute and all. But what if I hate myself?"

No one really had an answer aside from: "Try harder." Or, "If you do *this* program correctly, that won't be a problem anymore!" I'd throw myself into a program or book or eating plan and, when I was still miserable afterward, I'd fall prey to the lie that I had failed, or was inherently flawed and incapable of joy.

I remember sobbing on the floor one day, begging god or the creator of this simulation to "PLEASE JUST LET ME LEAVE." I had been working so hard on "loving myself" but was still stuck inside this trap of hatred, panic, and shame. *Being alive felt like a punishment.* Then, I had a wild thought: "What if I'm not flawed; what if the goal is?"

Self-love was an impossible goal for me because I was consumed by self-hatred. I didn't *consciously* desire to hate, bully, or harm myself. It felt like a program or computer virus was running rampant in my brain that I couldn't control.

So there I was, following guidance to look at myself in the mirror and say "I love you and forgive you" eleventy times. Then I'd hate myself more because I knew the affirmation was a lie. I mean, *I had tried to kill myself.* I did not love — nor did I forgive — myself.

Imagine being in a life-long relationship with someone who constantly bullied you or even tried to harm you.

Really think about it. Then, imagine that person suddenly decides that they're just gonna love you now. Hooray...

Would you immediately trust their refreshed, loving intentions? I wouldn't! It would be a long journey of rebuilding trust. *That's the same way it has worked in my relationship with myself.*

If self-love is the destination, we have a few other stops on the way.

Disliking the self is better than hating the self. Tolerating the self is better than disliking the self. Liking is better than tolerating, and so on.

So if anything remotely resembling self-love makes you want to curl up inside yourself until you become a teeny armadillo hiding inside a teeny armadillo shell, that's fine. Truly. Yeet[8] self-love to the curb for now. That's what I did. I had to.

If self-love seems forever far away for you, why not make self-tolerance your goal instead?

Adjust the knob

If something I recommend in this book feels unreachable for you, good. *Good.* That means there's room for growth. You have a starting point!

If a subsection's recommendation is too overwhelming, try this: Imagine a volume control knob on the subsection. Turn that little booger *down* until you find a "quieter" (less overwhelming) version of the recommendation that seems attainable. If the subsection recommends you *angrily dance* and that feels way out of reach, for example, turn the "knob" down to maybe... *bobbing your head to music* instead. A little something is better than a lot of nothing.

---

[8] This is a term the Youths use to denote "throwing." Upon questioning a Youth in my life, I discovered that the past tense is most likely "yeeted." *The more you know.*

Similarly, you can turn the volume UP on a recommendation, if you'd like. Get curious and find what works for you.

A little uncomfortable and a little scary is okay as we heal and grow, but painful and terrifying isn't the vibe we're going for here.

In yoga classes, they share advanced-level poses and *also* share the gentler, beginner poses. There are even adjustments people can make to their pose if they're compensating for an injury. *This* is just like *that*.

The floss trick

My healing journey started with a floss pick.

Ten years ago, if I'd read this book from beginning to end, I would have melted into a puddle of overwhelm. I'd have assumed that I needed to do ALL of the book's recommendations ALL at once. Nope. That's not the case at all.

There are folks who comment on my online videos about pursuing my big dreams, saying things like: "This is easier for you than it is for me. I could never do what you're doing. I can barely get out of bed."

I mean, yeah. I can get out of bed each day *now*. But years ago, I sure as shoot-dang couldn't. I'd go weeks without showering. I wailed and cried every day. Being alive was hell. I was afraid to close my eyes, even, because I felt *in my body* that I was always about to be attacked by someone or something. It's one of the reasons I hated showering, because I had to close my eyes to wash my face.

My point is: I may be doing all sorts of cool things with my life now, but I'm still that same Jen who was always one wrong look away from a panic attack. I'm simply further along on my journey now. And I'm still learning, healing, and growing.

Even though I hated being alive, I really wanted to *want to* be alive. I wanted to learn to engage with life and see if maybe, just maybe, it could be a bit less miserable. So, I started small. *Very small.*

I started by flossing my teeth each day, from bed, with a minty floss pick.

That's it. That's all I required of myself for that day. The next day, I did the same thing: wake up, floss pick, go back to sleep. After a few days, something pretty rad happened: **I was able to get out of bed and wash my face.** A couple weeks into my daily floss pick habit, I found myself taking a shower *without a preceding meltdown.*

Momentum is our friend on this healing journey. We need to meet ourselves where we are and right-size our self-care tasks to what is *attainable* and *sustainable.*

You don't get extra credit in life for overwhelming your system with a bunch of changes all at once. As you read through a section, consider finding and implementing *one* resonant thing. Just one.

If we add lots of new things all at once and start to feel more balanced, we have no way of knowing *which* of the added self-care tools helped!

Further, each section has around 10 subsections with various recommendations, some of which *may seem to contradict each other.* I have learned that each day is different. Some days I need gentle TLC, and other days I need a motivational fire under my buns. I don't think there's any single "answer" that we can implement and do every day forever and ever, never having to change it for the rest of our lives. Our needs evolve, and our capacity, mood, and stock of dark chocolate change daily. The varying guidance in the subsections hopefully makes space for those fluctuations.

Taking small, consistent steps will get us further in life than making giant leaps, collapsing into burnout, and avoiding everything for a month.

I do hope you learn how to balance your volume settings so you can engage with daily life and share your unique weirdness with the world. I know it's tough to experience life as deeply as we do. But, hey, no one else can appreciate the beauty of bird barf like we can. So, let's make the best of it.

CHOOSE YOUR OWN ADVENTURE

(emotional regulation style)

Now, the really fun part! This chunk of *Volume Control* has bite-sized tips, tricks, and doodles tailored to each emotional state. All you have to do is flip to the section that most resonates with how you currently feel, and start reading.

1

MELTDOWN

(alarms going off in head)

"This isn't worth it."

"LiFE has always been
and will always be this
hard. I can't do this. It's
not fair."

- JEN at a l

*Dear Jen at a **1**:*

Hey, kiddo.

Keep breathing.

Deep, belly breaths. It'll calm your central nervous system and get some feel-good chemicals to counteract the cortisol and adrenaline coursing through your body.

Seriously. It's science.

Take a deep breath. Then another one. Big, long exhales.

The tips and tricks in this section are short and to the point. I know it's a miracle for you to be reading this right now. That's already progress.

Thank you,** by the way. Thank you for making the effort to read this. **Thank you for refusing to give up.

The trick is to refuse to act on it.

There's this song by *The Spill Canvas* called "Self-Conclusion." I've listened to it many times when in the Ouch. The lyrics are on point: "You see the trick is that you're never supposed to act on it / No matter how unbearable this misery gets."

If you're in the Ouch right now, **your one job is to survive**, and to do so without acting on any self-destructive urge. At the very least, promise yourself that, just for today, you'll stay. Just for today, you won't hurt yourself. Then, revisit tomorrow.

Breathe. Busy yourself. Sleep. Binge-watch *Queer Eye* on Netflix. Sob in a giant heap on the floor. Vacuum a lot (or not at all). Play Yahtzee on your phone. Whatever it takes to not harm yourself or others, do that. **Stay.** This Storm *will* pass.

It's okay to be messy.

I need the reminder that it's okay to be a shitshow sometimes. I put so much pressure on myself to be everything to everyone, even on days when I can hardly get out of bed. I try to put on my mask of put-togetherness, even though I'm barely functioning.

So, here it is: It's okay to get messy. To fall apart. To feel like a blob of nothing on the kitchen floor where nothing makes sense, and you're certain that the missing oven mitt is the worst thing that's happened to anyone ever. It's okay.

It's okay if you don't shower today — though you'll feel better (or at least smell better) if you do — and it's okay if you merely exist under your weighted blanket in your ratty old fart pajamas.

You're a champion for surviving times like this.

Give yourself a break and allow yourself space to be however you are. Even if you're judging yourself, that's okay. *Try not to judge yourself for judging yourself.* Don't fight anything that's happening right now. Let Future You handle it. Right now, ride the wave. Let it splash. Let yourself be messy.

There's no need to take any action right now, aside from breathing. Focus on extended exhales. Breathe in that unique aroma of your fart jammies. **Breathe out the Suck.**

You're not alone or a burden.

When someone says, "You're not alone!" or "I'm here for you!" to me when I'm on the Struggle Bus, I want to kick them in their stupid, showered, emotionally-regulated shins. But I can't, obviously, because leaving the bed feels impossible. Also, I don't want them to be mad at me. I'm a lover, not a fighter.

I know the "you're not alone" phrase is cliché and can feel overused to the point of having zero meaning. But this isn't one of those "I'm here for you" blanket statements in a condescending, breathy voice. I'm speaking facts.

I know from experience that it's easy to feel all alone, like a victim of life, and to feel embarrassed or shameful for feeling so helpless. Silly bear; *that's like someone feeling ashamed of a chest cold.*

Everybody has had diarrhea at least once. Even Albert Einstein had diarrhea. Everyone has had an embarrassing moment and has told a joke that sucked. What's my point? *You are human. So are they.* We may see their put-togetherness and compare our messy behind-the-scenes to their highlight reels. But guess what, my little sweet potato? They get messy, too. Everyone does.

I think that's one of the biggest challenges, especially in the days of social media. With proper lighting and a couple of filters, I can look like a photoshopped model. In real life, I have ample toe hair and am poking at the zits on my face, sinking into existential despair because I've suddenly realized that one day the wall in my house will no longer be here and that's just sad. *It's such a good wall.*

So, yeah. It may be easy to think you're all alone and that you're a burden. But take it from me, the Ample Toe Hair Lady: *You're a human being doing your best to survive a Storm.* That's all this is. You are not alone. I know this for a literal real-life fact because I also experience life this way. I pinky promise you there is another someone out there who experiences life just like you do. If nothing else, stay put for *them*, so they too can feel less alone.

Also, **breathe**.

Don't make drastic decisions.

It's imperative to avoid big, life-changing reactions while in this space. I say this as someone who has quit multiple jobs and left many relationships while in the Suck. Only to later go: "Oh no. What did Meltdown Jen do this time?!" And then have to go into cleanup mode.

When it comes down to it, the desire to *hurry up and do something* is a desire for immediate relief from the discomfort. But I've learned this delightful and unfortunate truth: Discomfort is often what yields growth (Ew, gross, I know). Numbing this pain would just kick the can for Future You to deal with.

If you're feeling the itch to do something big or drastic or out of character, write down the actions you want to take or the ideas you have, and revisit them once the Brain Storm has passed. That way, you'll know the decision is from a place of grounded stability rather than panic.

A general rule of thumb I have is: if I'm actively considering hurting myself or pulling the plug on aspects of my life, *perhaps I'm not in the best mindset to trust other urges right now.*

I like using the 48-hour rule, especially if there's a big decision I want to make, an expensive item I suddenly want to purchase, or a relationship I want to end. Table the topic for 48 hours. Normally, after time away, the original sense of urgency leaves with the Storm. And I'm like: "Phew. I'm very glad I didn't blow up my life. Good work, Past Jen."

Make a circle of safety.

A **1** headspace can amplify a sense of overwhelm to the point that I become completely immobilized, which is when I normally find myself on the floor. My therapist[9] says this is me literally grounding myself. I like that description better than: "This is me failing as a human being because I can't even get up to walk to the bathroom."

I once worked with a self-proclaimed emotional healer who told me I could successfully quit my antidepressant medication by "envisioning dopamine flooding my brain." I was roughly six months sober and in an **11** (King of the world) headspace when she told me that. Naturally, I was like: "Yeah! That sounds totally feasible, healthy, and scientifically sound."

So, I abruptly stopped the medication that had essentially saved my life. Spoiler alert: Weeks later, I found myself in the kitchen holding a giant knife, about to plunge it into my chest.

I felt like I was under attack internally and externally, but not by anything I could physically see. I kept pleading for help, though I wasn't sure who or what I was asking. I was truly desperate.

Seemingly out of nowhere, I felt compelled to sit on the kitchen floor and draw an imaginary circle around myself.

---

[9] Sup, Amy!

So, I did. Though, through my tears and floor-level perspective, it likely looked more like an awkward peanut shape.

I then said aloud: "I'm staying in here until I no longer want to kill myself."

I ended up lying down, in my tiny oblong of safety, until the intensity lessened. The circle was a holding cell to keep me safe from, well, myself. Or whatever was steering the vehicle of myself during that terrifying time.

Obviously, you can replace "kill myself" with whatever you struggle with. Maybe it's: "I'm staying in here until I no longer want to leave my husband who's actually an amazing person, but I *really* want to blow up my life right now." Or, "I'm staying here until I no longer want to eat an entire jar of peanut butter in one sitting because I know it'll give me the worst belly ache."

What's your circle of safety? Maybe it's a bathtub, a closet, or under a weighted blanket. Maybe it's surrounded by cats and their precious toe beans. Find it, deem it a safe zone, and take a breather.

Oh, and please be kind to your brain. Some of us may need meds to get through rough times of life, **and that's okay**. It's taken me years to feel comfortable saying that, and I almost published the book without mentioning this. But this is my story and my truth. I hope it helps you.

Ask for help, ya stubborn bean.

When a Brain Storm hits, I want to hide from everyone. My comfort zone is isolation. I used to think I was saving people pain and trouble by hiding from them when I struggled. Turns out, my isolation and hiding *were often hurtful to them*. Makes sense, when I think about it. If someone hides from me when they're struggling, I feel like *I've* done something wrong, or like they don't trust me.

Apparently, the most loving thing I can do — for everyone involved — is to be honest. Share. If I don't yet feel safe sharing with a human, I can record my voice on my phone and go back and listen to it when in a **6** or above headspace. I can write in the notebook pages of this book and trust that Future Jen will read and respond with her guidance. I can talk to my dog, or even a rubber ducky[10]. Or a therapist, *which is like a friend that we pay.*

You may be in that mindset of: "But there's no one. I have no friends." If that's the case (or seems like the case right now), there is text and online support[11]. There are 12-step meetings. Community exists, even if we struggle to see it or are afraid of it. And, if that's all too overwhelming right now, there's always a composition notebook and a pen, or a text document.

Obviously, priority goes to talking with humans. Oh, and according to my partner, it's preferable to talk to *alive* humans rather than dead ones (beggars can't be choosers, Matt). If you've created a code word and shared it with loved ones (page 198) and you're on the verge of a crisis, **this may be a great time to use that code word.**

I recognize it can take a while to build a healthy support team of people who accept us for everything we are and who don't immediately want to shove us into a psych ward for being ourselves. This takes time and effort. It just does.

Reaching out to real-life, alive humans was challenging for me at first, and still can be. But please, do it. Even a text saying: "Hey I'm struggling a bit today. Will you send me some fun GIFs?" Just let someone else in the world know

---

[10] Some programmers keep a rubber ducky on their desk! If they run into an issue, they discuss it with Ducky before going to a manager. The solution often becomes clear just by speaking the issue aloud!
[11] Text or call 988 (U.S. only), or visit https://988lifeline.org/chat/

how you are. (Ask how they're doing, too!) If you're lucky, you'll receive the GIF of that dude tossing glitter in the air or the tiny owl saying "Aww yiiss."

AWW YIISS...

Isn't that better than feeling like you're drowning in the sea of all these human feelings?

Oftentimes, people will want to help "fix" it. This is how we're programmed, and their response is no indication of you being broken or unbearable in your current state. This is when you get to say:

"I don't need you to do anything. I just need space to be exactly as I am right now[12]."

---

[12] This is one of the most powerful sentences I've learned. Sometimes I need guidance. Other times, compassion. I'm learning to decipher which one I need and express that info to Earth human loved ones.

Also, please remember that it's no one's job to fix this. *There's nothing to fix.* You're in the middle of a Brain Storm, and it will pass. It reminds me of when I try to take the dog outside to go pee pee during a rainstorm. He looks at me like: "Um. Turn off the sky water, Food Lady." And I'm like, "Bro. I can't." Same thing applies here: Sometimes, we just gotta let the Storm run its course.

If you find yourself spiraling out to where life appears warped and scary, like you're looking through funny mirrors? You and your Supporter can try the "Real or not real?" trick in the +1 Supporter subsection (page 65).

Asking for help is one of the strongest things anyone can do. Hiding and isolating comes from a place of fear and pride. Stop that nonsense. Reach out to someone you love or to a helpline if need be.

You've got this.

Give it a silly hat.

If you deal with scary visualizations or thoughts, this subsection may help you get the upper hand in those storylines. I used to be inundated with twisted, scary images of me dying in various ways. *Y'know, creatively terrifying visuals that would make my therapist wide-eyed.*

One day, on a particular horror-genre kind of brain day, my mind was playing a visual of a scary demon monster attacking me. I started to have a panic attack, but then — I had an idea. What if I dress him in a silly outfit? It is *my* mind, after all. Shouldn't I be able to make tweaks to the visuals? So I did.

I gave the demon a silly hat.

In my mind, in the visual of the horrible thought, I reached in and changed it. *The demon didn't look so scary anymore.* The storyline of the thought itself even paused like: "Wtf? This wasn't part of the script."

Then, I made the silly-looking demon dance[13].

This is a sneaky, quirky, at times funny way to show myself that I am not my thoughts, and that I do retain some creative rights when it comes to rewriting crappy storylines.

---

[13] This was originally inspired by the boggart-banishing spell "Riddikulus!" in *Harry Potter*.

If you aren't a visual person, perhaps you hear gnarly, intrusive thoughts in your mind. The same storyline rewriting trick can work with thoughts.

Here's a real-life example.

The thought in my head was: "You're driving with your partner's kids in the car. What if another car crashes into you and then everyone dies except for you?! What a miserable life that will be!"

I caught the thought and made it absurdly ridiculous: "What if instead, our cars turn into balloon animals and gravity ceases to exist and we all float around getting hit in the face by saggy boobs? What a wild life that will be!"

The writing crew in my Intrusive Thought department was like...

The beauty of a bizarre approach like this is that it's weird enough to yank us out of our minds and into our bodies. From there, we can get a bit more control of the amped up volume of our **1** headspace. Also, I normally make myself chuckle, which is a miracle in a **1** state.

So what if you "know better"?

Sometimes, I start spinning out because I'll logically know that life itself is fine, but my present-moment feelings don't match that knowledge. Rationally, I understand that episodes will pass. I know that I'll soon feel more comfortable. And, since I have that knowledge, I'll beat myself up over not *handling this better*. I'll convince myself not to reach out to anyone, telling myself: "This will be over soon, so you may as well save yourself the trouble and embarrassment."

But, bottom line, when I'm in the Suck... I'm in it. When you're in the Suck, you're in it. *This is happening now*. **Deal with the lessons and logic later.** Right now, feeding thoughts with more thoughts is not helpful. Judging yourself for being an imperfect human isn't helpful. What *is* helpful is a bit of grace. Support. A sprinkle of patience.

If you had a friend who was feeling lousy, would you berate them for feeling that way? Remind them they should feel differently? Tell them to snap out of it? Ideally not. You'd likely be supportive or at least sympathetic. So, take it easy on yourself. **Further stressing your brain will not make this go by any faster.** Being *gentle* will.

Let Future You deal with the figuring-out portion of all this. Clarity is always easier in hindsight once the Storm has passed.

Grandma Google isn't a doctor.

Listen, I know we're in the age of self-diagnosis and that a resonant diagnosis can be very helpful. But right now? In this current alarm-going-off, fight-or-flight, "AAAHHHH" state? Consider postponing the rabbit hole of asking Grandma Google to diagnose you. She'll still be there tomorrow, or next week.

I got lost on that path for many years. Sometimes, I still find it tempting when I'm experiencing a gnarly Brain Storm.

The deep, mucky darkness can make it seem like reality has always been this painful, *which must mean something is wrong with me.* Thus, the most immediate way to get an answer to why life is so hard for me is to find a name for it. (Cue Grandma Googs.) Then, I'd come away with multiple labels for feeling as deeply as I felt. Shit, I got over ten diagnoses from doctors even before doing a swan dive[14]

---

[14] It looked oddly like a cannonball, but I definitely felt like a swan.

into Google. Each doctor would say the previous one was incorrect, and give me a new, fresh label.

I remember loving the title of "treatment-resistant depression." I was like, *Yeah! I'm so broken that no one can fix me. Ha! I'm special! Even doctors are baffled! Everyone, come marvel at how messed up I am!*

Part of me really enjoyed being sick, being stuck. There was no accountability in that space. While it sucked and was painful, it was a comfortable pain. I realize now that I was using my slew of diagnoses to stay stuck. Frankly, it was easier that way.

Maybe we are our diagnoses. Or, maybe we are sensitive people who were not properly taught how to feel and handle emotions (because our guardians didn't know what the heck they were doing either), and now we are learning how to regulate. Hey, maybe we're all the above.

I'm not discrediting all doctors or diagnoses. I am, however, strongly urging against using *the internets* as your freelance physician. You'll walk away thinking you have testicular cancer of the middle finger, or something. Don't try to figure this out right now. Just breathe and take care of yourself. Okay? The basics, like water and food. Put on fresh socks if you're feeling froggy. Save the psychology deep dive for later.

If you must Google something, Google funny cat videos.

Grandma Googs is great at those.

If you were supposed to be dead...

...you'd be dead already.

The fact that you're alive is evidence that you still have shit to learn and joy to experience. And yes, more pain to feel. And then more realizations to come from said pain.

Circle of life and all that.

AAAHHHsaaveenyaa bag of peaches maammaa

An ex of mine once said: "What if you're set to win the lottery in five years? You'll never know if you die now."

He had a point. *Great guy. Not great boyfriend.*

The good news is we're all gonna die anyway. *throws confetti* So, how about you stop trying to control the process and just let life happen? Some cool stuff is gonna happen. Some lame stuff is gonna happen. Then, ideally more coolness. And a lot of boring in-betweens. And then, you'll die.

The end.

Credits roll.

When you're dead, you won't be able to do things like drink cold water on a hot day, eat your favorite dessert, or come up with dramatic backstories for strangers while stuck in traffic. You won't be able to properly marvel at the beauty of bird barf.

Death is the one guarantee in life. So, until then, *chill out.*

Oh, and **breathe**[15].

Wiggle your finger.

There are times when I quite literally cannot move. My brain tells my body to do a thing, and my body is like, "LOLNO." My internal wires get crossed or something. This total lack of control often induces panic or adds to the story that there's *most definitely* something wrong with me.

If you know, you know.

To an outsider, I probably look like a SIMs character caught in a glitch, trying so hard to do something as simple as get out of bed.

If a person doesn't experience this sort of thing, they may squint their eyes in confusion and be like: "Just get up."

---

[15] There are like 703 reminders to "breathe" in this book. I genuinely don't think I learned to properly breathe until I was in my thirties. My default state was holding my breath. Our brains need oxygen!

There are two approaches that work best for me when I'm *stuck*.

The first is to **wiggle a finger**. I stop focusing on all the things I "ought" to be doing and stop trying to move my entire body. Instead, I bring my entire focus to only one of my fingers. Or, as a follower calls them, *tickle sticks*.

So, let's try it. Bring all your focus into one finger/tickle stick. Maybe it's your pointer finger, or maybe it's your middle "I love you, stranger[16] in traffic who's driving poorly" finger. Doesn't matter. Pick one.

Now, focus all your energy on moving that one finger. It may be slow at first, but it should at least shimmy a bit. This can take a minute or so for me sometimes, as if my brain's electrical impulses are reorganizing just to get this little bit of movement.

Once that finger has some decent movement, let the other fingers join the party. Do a tame version of spirit fingers, wiggling them all around. *Even this is a win*, and you're welcome to stop here if you'd like. If you want to continue, go ahead.

Next, move your wrist.

Then, your elbow.

Then, your shoulder.

You get how it works? We're overcoming inertia by applying a tiny little wiggly-finger force. We're slowly but surely building momentum from that tiny movement. Keep the momentum going until you can inch out of bed. Keep moving, or celebrate the victory by taking a nap.

If this first option doesn't work (and it normally does), here's Phase II. Rather than swimming in the sludge of panic trying to change the current situation, I just give into it. I accept that, currently, for whatever reason, my body is

---

[16] My guess is his name is Chartreuse... and he goes by Char... and his dream is to be a professional juggler... but his dead-beat uncle stole all his juggling savings! So now Char is super cranky in traffic. :-(

grounded where it is. **I stop fighting.** I breathe and relax and allow myself to lay there like a bump on a log or a very sleepy squirrel on the side of the road. I just... exist. And allow. The first few times I tried this, it took a while for the spinning thoughts to calm down – to stop panicking that my body wasn't doing what I wanted, and thinking: *Oh crap, maybe it never will.*

When I stop putting all my energy and focus into *fighting* my current experience and instead accept, "Welp. This is where I am right now." And relax into it? Eventually (it normally doesn't take long), I'll find myself effortlessly getting out of bed without even thinking about it.

If you have another approach that works for you, there's some notebook paper in a few pages. Add your notes there (or here, if you'd like).

Leave it to Future You.

You're likely not in much of a problem-solving space right now. If your volume knob is turned way up, life is probably way too loud to focus on solutions or to see life or your situation clearly. So, don't try to fix anything right now. Don't try to figure anything out or take drastic steps. Just take one little baby step at a time to survive *right now.* Trust that Future You will have more clarity, because life won't be quite as loud for them.

This is an especially helpful approach for me when I'm stressed about all the things I need to do or will ever have to do. As if the tasks and projects *all need to be completed or figured out right now.* I'll be in a **1** headspace, barely able to move, yet spiraling over everything I should be doing. *Just should-ing all over the darn place.*

So I'll pause and remind myself that Future Me will be in a much better headspace to take care of this stuff. The tasks and projects aren't going anywhere. They'll still be here tomorrow.

I was suspicious of this exercise at first, but it really does help. It encourages my brain to let out a sigh of relief.

Also, now is a great time to write a note to Future You. You can use the notebook paper at the end of this section, a note-taking app on your phone, or whatever else tickles your pickle. I share specific approaches in the **"How to make your own"** section at the end of the book that can help spark that conversation between your Stormy Self and Sunny Self. During the Suck, I recommend trying *the two-way radio approach* (page 324).

And for now, in a **1** headspace, maybe just give yourself space to be an unspiritual, temper tantrum shitshow. Write from that place. Be uninhibitedly honest. *Here's how I feel. Here's what I'm thinking. Here's what I need. Here's what I want to do that I probably shouldn't.* And so on.

Then, give yourself the rest of the day off from trying to fix or figure anything out. Just chill, butter bean.

+1: Real or not real?

*Your loved one's current state: **1 (Meltdown)***

Hello, trusted Supporter. Your Sensitive loved one is having a rrough time right now. They may not be aligned with reality and are instead swept up in fear, overwhelm, or sadness. They may need your help deciphering what's real and what's not. *Here's what I mean.*

My trusted Supporter is my partner. He calls himself my "toe tether." He jokes that he must tie a string to my toe and hold onto the other end, to prevent me from sinking too low or flying too high.

He also helps me when I lose a bit of my grasp on reality. When my volume is MAXed out, it's hard for me to tell the difference between fear and intuition. My panicked brain could be screaming the most dramatic, out-there story, and if I'm at a **1** or **2**, I will likely believe it as truth.

One of my favorite movies is *The Hunger Games*[17]. Without spoiling anything for folks who've yet to watch it, one main character gets his brain all scrambled and hijacked by the bad guys. As a result, he can't tell what's real and what's not. He thinks his friends are his enemies and enemies are his friends, and he feels like a crazy person. *My view of life during a 1 can feel very similar.*

While he unravels the twisted knot of his psyche, he starts asking his trusted loved ones: "Real or not real?"

When he can't tell the difference between reality and his panicked mind, he asks. Then, he trusts his loved ones' responses as truth.

I do this with my partner. I'll plop face-first on the bed and say: "I feel like you hate me because I'm sad and unshowered, and you'd rather be with someone substantially more stable and calm than me. Real or not real?" He'll smile and chuckle in the precious, loving way only he can and reply: "Very not real. I don't want the stable, calm person. She sounds boring. I want you."

---

[17] Yes, I'm now aware it was a book first. No, I didn't know that at the time I watched the movies. Yes, I'm eternally sorry to have failed you, my darling book worms.

If your Sensitive loved one seems to be viewing life via funny mirrors, it may be helpful to ask them what their current view of reality is. "What's going on in your brain? What sort of wild stories is your brain telling you?"

From there, encourage them to trust you when you tell them *real* or *not real*. And please be honest. If they're intuiting that something is *off* with you, don't say "not real" just to avoid what would otherwise be a sweaty, uncomfortable 15-minute conversation to clear the air.

This process doesn't have to be stressful, though it might feel awkward at first. Building trust takes time. My partner and I now laugh as I tell him the *highly dramatic* stories swirling around my mind when I'm at a **1**.

If you'd like, here's a spot to jot down notes:

SUPPORTER NOTES

2

BARELY HANGING ON

(might lose shit at any moment)

"Is this even worth it?"

"Noises are so loud and make my skin feel like it's crawling off my body. The volume knob on all my sensitivities is cranked up and I feel like I can't fix it. I keep trying to do things to "feel better," but nothing is catching hold. I'm trying to climb, but the rock wall is smooth, or it keeps moving like a treadmill. I feel like I am doing all the "right things" without making progress. I feel like I'm pulling a piano through quicksand. I'm honestly to a point where I don't even care enough to feel better. I'm just sort of... surviving."

— JEN at a 2

*Dear Jen at a **2**:*

I love that you said "surviving," because that's really your only responsibility right now. This section has some perspective shifts and analogies to help curate a wee bit of self-compassion. Do your best to get through those. But when it comes down to it? Your only goal is to stay, and to refuse to hurt yourself or others. You've got this, love. You've survived worse. Don't give up.

The key is to stay put.

So, you feel like crap. Maybe your skin feels like it's crawling off your body or is too tight. You could be yearning for home without knowing where "home" is. Perhaps you're struggling to breathe and feel like your throat is closing. Or you're being inundated with scary, twisted thoughts that would even make your therapist clutch her pearls.

You're *in it*, my friend. *In the Suck.*

And I know the go-to is to try and find a panic button. When the internal alarms start blaring, I become frantic to turn them off.

Sometimes, I can calm the panic with a few deep breaths with long exhalations, or a splash of water on my face. Other times, my experience is like a roller coaster. As desperate as I am to get off this ride, *sometimes I have to let it run its course.*

The key is to stay put. Stay here on Earth, of course. But also... do what you can to stay present rather than trying to run from or numb what you're feeling. It's that annoying and equally true statement: *Wherever you go, there you are.* Even if you run away, your Ouch comes with.

Think of it like trying to run from a thunderstorm so you don't get wet, all the while running in the same direction the storm is moving!

Stay put, breathe, take care of one little task at a time. The Suck will leave just as it came. Maybe in twenty minutes, maybe in two days, or longer. But, no matter what, it'll pass. And the more comfortable you get sitting in the discomfort of challenging emotions, the faster they'll pass.

It takes practice, but I've found that there is a surprising amount of power in relaxing into the Ouch. It gives the Ouch energy a chance to move *through* us, rather than hang around and harden inside our bodies. So, please don't run away! I like you here!

Go sit on Mars.

My brain can hyperfocus on a tiny detail, zoom way in on it, and make it appear giant. And I rarely find myself hyperfocusing on positive things. It's normally painful stuff or an obsession with my next creative project (which conveniently arrives at 1AM on a Tuesday). Or my brain will choose to hyperfocus on the fact that I have a little cushion under my chin, and if I angle my face a certain way it's like I have a quadruple chin, and that's *just not fair*.

The vanity-based chin thought, for example, can take up my focus for an entire day. I recognize that this hyperfocus thought is totally self-absorbed. But, in the moment, I'm not consciously aware that I'm *choosing* this as my focus. It more so feels like the focus possesses me, which sucks. *Think of all the bird barf[18] I'm missing.*

---

[18] Callback to the intro. Out of context, this reference may be confusing. Maybe I should remove this footnote, though, and let you be confused. Then, you can hyperfocus on bird barf all day instead.

This hyperfocus mindset can make a Brain Storm, suicidal ideations, or the hypersensitive part of me seem giant. My brain takes *all* the past pain and confusion and applies it *all* to right now. Or, it takes every task I ever have to do and, rather than seeing them as something to accomplish one by one, I feel like all tasks must be done right now. All at the same time. All to an A+ standard.

Think of a field of grass. In a large, green field, imagine how many individual blades of grass there are. This current **2** emotional state is a tiny chunk of grass in that giant field (or maybe even the whole continent or planet). When we hyperfocus on our pain, our perspective becomes that of an ant. What is otherwise a tiny patch of grass suddenly appears giant and all-encompassing.

Ever since I was a kid, my dad has told me to zoom out and sit on Mars. "Then," he says, "You'll see how tiny these seemingly giant problems actually are." The goal isn't to avoid our problems. The goal is to right-size our point of view.

So, zoom out. This can feel unfamiliar or challenging the first handful of times you do it. It's like any other muscle or skill, though — it just takes practice.

What works for me is sitting in bed (yum), closing my eyes, and visualizing my body in the room I'm in. Then, I imagine zooming out to see the building I'm in.

I zoom out further to see the neighborhood. I normally pause here because, in my neighborhood currently, there are around 300 houses. That's at least 300 other people with seemingly giant grass blade problems, many of whom are likely struggling with something more dire than a quadruple chin.

Keep pressing that zoom-out button: your city, your state (or however geography works where you live), then your planet.

Check out Earth — it's so pretty! You can't even see your neighborhood anymore. No need to worry about that $50 fine from the neighborhood HOA (homeowners association) because they think clovers are weeds *but you demand to keep clovers to feed the bumblebees.*

Next, do an anti-gravity cartwheel out further to sit on Mars. Look back at Earth — it's so tiny!

. <- Representation of Earth from a Martian's POV[19].

---

[19] Their name is Max. We text on WhatsApp.

This exercise isn't to belittle your feelings; it's to shift your perspective for a bit. Oh, and when you're done, come back to Earth, please.

Something else that helps me realize just how small I am is to watch a space documentary. After hearing that there are trillions of galaxies in our observable universe and that each galaxy can have billions to trillions of stars, I tend to let go of my grip on whatever my current, teeny-tiny-by-comparison stressor is. *Psshht, I can handle this.*

What if you had a tummy bug?

Think about the last time you had a stomach virus. For a few days, a virus takes up a lot of mental, emotional, and physical space. It hijacks life a little bit. No one ever *plans* to get sick. No one is ever like: "Y'know what I'd like? Diarrhea to hit my belly guts in the middle of the Monday AM Zoom meeting right after Ed says 'let's circle back' for the ninth time."

If I regularly got tummy bugs, I'd make sure to have a care package, just in case. I'd have ginger root and digestive tea and whatever else helps. I'd tell my partner that ice water helps my tummy and so do belly rubs.

How is being in a challenging emotional state any different? It isn't. You don't feel well. It's as simple as that.

This shift in mindset often helps me find compassion for myself when I'm emotionally not feeling well. It's tough, because many of us were raised to believe that physical ailments were taken more seriously than emotional or mental ones. (I think this is why I historically have gotten super physically sick every six months, so I'd give my mind and body the rest it craved all along.)

This little tummy bug (or Brain Storm) is simply something you're experiencing in the moment. It's not forever, and it doesn't define you.

Dare to have a wee bit of compassion for yourself, yeah? *What would you say to me, or your pet?* Try saying that to yourself. Keep it simple and truthful.

I'm sorry you don't feel well.

Accept that the pain exists.

Every single time I go through an emotional Valley, it takes me to a deeper truth or realization about myself or about life. This may be hard to grasp in a **2** mindset, but it's proven true for me.

My go-to used to be to constrict around an uncomfortable feeling rather than allow myself to physically feel it. That approach doesn't get rid of the feeling, though – it just holds it in my body for Future Me to handle.

Now, when I catch myself holding my breath and tensing around an uncomfortable feeling, I stop and take the biggest breath I've taken all day. Then, I say: "Alright, (insert feeling here). I see you. I accept that you are currently visiting. What lesson did you bring me this time?" I focus on how the feeling physically feels in my meat suit and continue to breathe into it. And the discomfort lifts much, much faster.

I used to think that "acceptance" of a situation meant I was okay with it. *What if I'm in a really shitty situation that very much isn't okay?! Accepting a shitty situation is admitting defeat and giving up, right?* No. **The challenge is to accept *that* the pain currently exists.** I mean, it does exist. Right now, it's happening. A starting point is to *accept that*. We're not giving in to this reality for forever; we're simply recognizing how it is *right now*. This gives us a starting point.

Rather than try to fix the uncomfortable emotion or feel differently, dare yourself to coexist with the emotion. You don't have to be consumed by it. You can feel the feelings without your whole life being derailed. Just keep moving — little step by little step — and keep breathing. I promise you; some lovely realization is being birthed from within you.

Feel the feels in your body.

If your brain feels frantic or panicked right now, try this: *Feel it in your body.* Focus on the physical sensations in your beautiful sack of flesh. Breathe and allow yourself to sense how these emotions feel physically. Is there a burning in your chest? A weight on your shoulders? A pressure in your head? Does it all feel like, "AAAHHHH!" Great. Breathe into it. Allow it.

Is there a color, texture, or flavor of the emotion? Own it. And trust the process of feeling and witnessing these feelings. I once heard that emotion is "e-motion," standing for "energy in motion" – meaning that feelings are meant to be physically felt, *not thought*. This has been challenging for me because I like to intellectualize, rather than feel, my feelings.

The only way out is through. Breathe into what you're feeling, physically feel it in your body, and allow it to naturally dissipate. I promise it will, even if only a bit.

You're only the center of *your* universe.

It's such a lousy feeling, isn't it? Sending unanswered telepathic messages to a loved one (or *anyone)* to come help us, climb over our walls, and see through our fake smile? Or, what about when we do share that we're struggling and someone offers a platitude, seems indifferent, gets overwhelmed, or doesn't respond at all?

Are they a horrible, uncaring person?

Or are they possibly a human being with their own stressors and feelings, who maybe can't read your mind? And, even if they could read your mind, perhaps they're too exhausted from their own lives to drop everything and come to your aid. Human life is a heavy lift for everyone, not just highly sensitive folks.

Frankly: It is no one's responsibility to rescue you. That's too much to ask of any person. When we expect someone else to read our minds or miraculously know what we need, that's setting everyone up for failure. While you may be lucky enough to have intuitive loved ones who can sense when something is off, *it's not their responsibility to always take care of you.*

It is *your* responsibility to take care of you.

Right now, in a **2** mindset, the word "responsibility" may suck to hear. When I'm in a **2**, I'm barely hanging on, damnit. Someone help me – I feel like I'm drowning!

I think reaching out is imperative when in a Stormy spot. But we need to learn to be okay if someone is unable to (or chooses not to) show up to help us. I mean, if it's a recurring issue where someone only wants you when you're witty and showered and helpful, and they tend to ghost you if you have a bad day? Well, it's possible that they suck. And you may need to reevaluate that friendship. (But not now. Now is not the time for decisions. Right now is the time for survival. Table it for later.)

Do what you need to do to take care of yourself. Do unto yourself as you'd want others to do unto you. Wish a motherly person was here to make you soup? Make yourself soup, even if it's from a can. Wish someone would cuddle you and tell you everything is okay? Put on fuzzy socks, get a hot cup of tea, and snuggle yourself under a blanket, while whispering that everything is okay[20]. No matter how awkward it feels, do it.

It's easy to fall into victimhood and blame others for how we feel. I challenge you to reach out to your support team *and* be your own support, to the best of your ability. If soup and snuggles seem too far-fetched right now, that's okay. Maybe drinking a glass of water or taking a shower will be the self-care win for the day. That's great, too. Or just, like, put on some pants and stay alive. **Keep it simple.**

If you don't have a support team yet? That's okay. You will. I remember feeling like I'd never find my people. You know what happened? As I learned to allow myself to be *myself,* my people *found me.* The more I showed up for myself, the more I started to attract folks who also could show up for me. And I now have the capacity to show up for them, too, which is nothing short of a miracle.

---

[20] If you have kiddos at home, this may feel impossible. Pop on an audiobook or show for them, go into a dark closet, take three deep breaths. Whisper that it'll be okay. *Something is better than nothing.*

Remember that there are helplines. There is even an online chat where you can text a counselor[21]. There are support groups for all kinds of struggles. If that seems too overwhelming, there's a blank text document or journal that'd love to your uninhibited thoughts and feelings.

Take a belly breath, zoom out, and recognize that every single person in your neighborhood and town and state and country and planet occasionally struggles. You're not the center of the universe, and **you're not alone**.

If you stay.

One of my biggest fears is dying without my big dreams coming true. What if I die without writing a book that helps lots of people? Or without doing speaking events, or making a movie? I've had these dreams since I was a kid, even if the dreams felt out of reach for most of my life.

It's a good reminder to myself that *if I leave,* those most certainly won't come true. *If I stay,* there's a far better chance. Granted, nothing is a given. **But I'll certainly do a better job writing a book alive than I will dead.** My blog post being read by three people and positively impacting one person has a further reach than my thoughts and feelings *when I'm dead.*

You can use this as a writing prompt, even.

---

[21] Text or call 988 (U.S. only), or visit https://988lifeline.org/chat/

If I stay... I get to experience a bubble bath again. I'll likely have a laugh loop. Maybe I'll get lucky and see another naked fight scene with Viggo Mortensen.

Finish the prompt: "If I stay, at least I'll be able to..."

If this feels too challenging right now, save it for Future You when the Suck has lifted. Once you have this "if you stay" info, keep it somewhere where you can reference it during rough times. Add it to the back of this section, to sticky notes, or wherever works best for you.

If you leave.

I've learned to see suicidal thoughts, images, and urges as an alarm of some sort. *What is it that I'm missing? What is my body trying to tell me?* These questions are challenging to answer when in a **2** headspace. Here's a sneaky way to get the answer.

If next Monday was your last day here, what would you do in the meantime? Seriously, take a moment to think about it.

Here's mine: If I knew I was checking out Monday, I'd spend more time outside, paint, tell people I love them, make amends for wrongdoings, and write and share like my life depended on it.

So... why not do those things right now? (Assuming they're positive.)

Something about putting a make-believe deadline on life inspires a sudden clarity. I challenge you to try this. If you were gonna leave, what would you take care of first? How would your priorities shift? What can you do today to take an itty-bitty step toward these more pressing priorities?

I've found that this clarity feels like a tiny ray of sunshine peeking through the clouds. It's a sliver of inspiration during a time when everything feels dark and impossible.

Schedule your sulk.

Thankfully, most mornings I wake up and feel generally content. (This is a night-and-day difference from how I used to wake up, which was: Open eyes. Enjoy the glorious in-between-dream-and-awake state. Become conscious that I'm alive and have to do this life thing again. *Sob profusely.*)

There are still mornings when I wake up and life feels heavy, and...

I just.

Don't.

Wanna.

Something I've found to be helpful is to set my phone's timer for 15 minutes, and then fully fall into the sulk. But *only* for 15 minutes. That's the deal I make with myself.

I don't tell myself to snap out of it. I don't tell myself I have so much to be grateful for. And I also try not to fling to the other end of the extreme and lay in bed all day.

I grant myself permission to be in full-on sulk mode for 15 minutes. I whine. I complain. I flail. I have temper tantrums. I lay face-first on the floor and scream. Then, *I move on.*

Every single time I've done this, it's been helpful.

Having permission to be right where I am at that very moment, even if it's wanting to shave my head and hide under my covers forever, is freeing.

What happens if, for a predetermined amount of time, you give yourself permission to be exactly where you are and really lean into the feelings? Set a timer. Give it a try. Lean in, let go, and get messy with it. When the alarm goes off, splash some cold water on your face. Pat yourself on the back for a job well done.

Make the darn bed.

Okay, hear me out. I know that a **2** mindset can make everything seem insurmountable. Picking a task — any task — helps us gain forward momentum on something *aside from the inner workings of our mind*. Be as cranky as you want about it. This really does work. If not "make the bed," pick some other mundane task. Put the dishes away like the badass you are. Put on clean socks. Brush your teeth. Or floss with a floss pick.

If you're in a place where bed-making seems the equivalent of hiking Mount Everest in stilettos, then break it down into nibbles. Something like this:

1. Stand up.
2. Grab the pillow from the floor.
3. Put the pillow on the bed.

Once you've accomplished these tasks, make a mental note of the next few. Once those are done, allow yourself to celebrate this as a victory. (I like to text another Sensitive about my win and ask them to send GIFs of excitement.)

Only put-together people make their beds. You are *so* an adult right now.

If moving your body *at all* seems impossible right now, remember that you can start by wiggling your finger. Seriously. Put all your focus into that movement. Once the finger wiggles, wiggle the other fingers, and then focus on moving your hand. Your wrist. Then your arm. Eventually, the momentum will start to carry you.

Very slow movement is still movement.

Do things you know you enjoy.

I don't like doing things; I like *having done* things. Apparently, in order to have done something, we must first do it. Lame. LAME!

As you follow this guide through ups and downs, you'll ideally make a list of different things that you enjoy (which is a recommended to-do item for a 7 headspace, on page 222). *This* is the time to consult that list. If you're unable to make one in your current state, make a note for your Future Self to do so.

It is possible — likely, even — that none of the items on your list will currently seem intriguing to you at all. They normally don't for me. The only appetizing thing is to find a cave to slowly rot away in, or to hide under my weighted blanket and ignore everyone until they finally leave me alone. And then be miffed at them for not climbing over my walls, even though all I've done is push them away.

But let's be real. Is that what you want? Do you want to Eeyore[22] this, or do you want to take some forward action *even when* you feel lousy? I like to think of it as investing in my emotional bank account. If I'm in a **2** headspace, my account may be in the negatives. As such, I'll do the "enjoyable" activity, I'll hate every second of it, and then notice afterward that I'm feeling just a bit more... okay.

If you haven't made a list yet, perhaps pulling from mine on the next page can be helpful.

(Note that when I'm in a **1-5** mindset, these all sound as appetizing as garbage juice. But when I trust my Sunnier Self who made this list and I reluctantly do the thing, I always feel at least a tiny bit more like myself afterward. And yes, during a **2**, I find it immensely annoying when the simple, self-care exercise *actually works*.)

---

[22] Eeyore, the depressed donkey from A.A. Milne's childhood classic, *Winnie the Pooh*, is the greatest example ever of a **2** mindset. If you know where he is, please give him a copy of this book.

- Write, doodle, or paint.
- Walk or hike with the pup.
- Drink tea that's sippable hot-wise.
- Meditate. Shakti mat for extra credit.
- Light candles and huff essential oils.
- Read a book. Fairy smut permitted.
- Watch feel-good movies.
- Sit or stand barefoot on the earth.
- Bake.
- Do some yoga or light stretching.
- Solo excursions to the movie theater.
- Make fresh juice.
- Dance to a song. (Normally "I'm Still Standing" by Elton John.)
- Swing on a swingset.
- Remove trash from office or room.
- Crafts or any kind of DIY thing.
- Shower so I don't reek on top of also feeling like a depressed sloth.

When it comes down to it, our brains still have worn-in grooves of feeling lousy or sulky about this weird game called life. The enjoyable experiences may seem unattainable right now. It may seem like this current **2** state of being is all that's ever been, that it's always just been lurking under the surface.

Taking action steps that you *logically know* are enjoyable to you (even if they don't feel enjoyable in the moment) is one of the best ways to anchor into a less reactive state and stop or slow a downward spiral. These action steps also pay it forward for Future You.

So, pick one thing, and do it.

Even if you don't feel immediately more comfortable, you can at least write the item on your to-do list *and then cross it off*. Oh, the gratification.

Help someone else.

Not eleven minutes ago, I was blowing tears and snot into a rough-feeling paper towel because I couldn't find any soft and fluffy tissues because life was *that unfair* in the moment. I was totally questioning my relationship and my place in the world and why skin even exists. I sat down to reference the guidance I'd previously offered in this section. I read it and it helped, and then I was like, "Ooo. You know what I could really use a reminder of right now?" *Out poured five more pages of material.*

See, a benefit to experiencing these sticky lows is that I know I can show up for others when they're in a similar place. Keeping track of how I feel and what I want (and what I *need*, which is often different from the want) lets me empathize with others when they're struggling. I couldn't have made this guidebook unless I'd first experienced a tremendous amount of pain. I can use that pain to help others. Together, *we can make something beautiful with our pain.*

Through my experience, I've learned I don't want someone to tell me I'm wrong for feeling the way I feel or to tell me to snap out of it. I also don't want someone to co-sign my bullshit and let me sit in a pile of sweaty, stinky victimhood for a week. All I want is someone to read my mind and tenderly dance on the tightrope of what I need. *Is that so much to ask?* (Sigh. Apparently so.)

So, I write down how I feel during my **2's** and **3's**. I make note and do my best to remember the dance between *needing to feel heard* and *needing help getting out of the Suck*. Then, I can implement this knowledge in a pay-it-forward kind of way. To myself and to others.

I recommend reaching out to three people you know and asking how their day is going. That's it. Just listen. Sometimes, I feel exhausted after doing this. Other times, there'll be an amazing conversation where one of us offers the same guidance and support that we individually needed. (Life is sneaky like that.) There are moments I get pumped because the person I called didn't answer and I got their voicemail instead. *I leave excellent voicemails.*

If the person is one of those nonstop talkers who drinks your energy with a twisty straw, don't call them. Choose easier conversationalists.

The goal here is to step outside of ourselves for a bit. This can help us realize that we are not at all alone in our pain or struggle. Being human is freaking tough! The goal is *not*, however, to pour ourselves into helping others to avoid our own shit. We just need to stop hyperfocusing on ourselves for a bit, that's all.

Another fun thing to do is donate a wee bit of money[23]. I recently went to Aldi (a grocery store) and a woman gifted me her shopping cart. The carts there normally cost 25 cents, so it wasn't a costly favor for her. Yet I felt (and acted) like I'd just been given a toilet made of solid gold. Honestly, I'm fairly certain I scared her with how excited I was. *I'm not sorry.*

Buy someone's beverage at a coffee place or share an honest compliment with a person in your life. Do something kind for another. I've learned through recovery groups that we gain self-esteem by doing "esteemable" acts. It's one of those sayings that annoys me because it is *so true.* I mean, we obviously don't need to exhaust ourselves by pouring from an empty emotional cup. The goal isn't huge, sweeping motions, but rather small, sustainable ones.

No one knows what they're doing.

I went through most of my life thinking that everyone else had a guidebook to life that I simply wasn't given. My

---

[23] But only what you can spare. The goal is tiny steps, like a $3 donation. Let's not overdraft our accounts.

basic state of being could be defined as "ostracized." I felt alone, weird, and like I had lobster claws for hands while everyone else had magical fingers that could probably play the saxophone really well.

The older I've gotten, the more I've realized the truth: *We're all clueless.* And oftentimes, the folks who *seem* the most put-together are compensating for how much of an unresolved shitshow they are on the inside.

So, please do not compare your behind-the-scenes to the opening night show they're putting on. Their show may seem well-rehearsed, their outfit and words meticulously chosen. But if you pulled back the curtain, you'd see that they're messy, too.

+1: This isn't a math problem.

Your loved one's current state: **2 (Barely hanging on)**

Hello, Supporter. Your loved one is struggling. First and foremost, *you haven't done anything wrong.* I say this because I know my partner used to take my Struggle Bus times personally. This extra subsection is simply to offer *another way of looking at the current* **2** *situation.*

We, as humans, like to fix problems. That's often how we show love or offer help. However, when it comes to a fellow human's emotional state, *there's nothing for you to fix.* There's nothing to solve. No sneaky algebraic equation or alphanumeric passcode will suddenly stop someone's sensitivities or "snap them out of" a Brain Storm. In fact, other's eagerness to help me "feel better" often results in me shutting down or detaching from that person even more.

Someone giving me space to be exactly as I am without pressuring me to feel or think differently, on the other hand, tends to help the Brain Storm pass faster.

I say this because, to Supporters, the solution may seem simple. "Just go for a run!" "Don't be anxious!" "Do yoga!" "Take these supplements!" "Huff essential oils!" "Find Jesus!" "Make a gratitude list!" "Eat more veggies!"

I know for me, at a **1** or **2**, I don't want you to tell me how to fix the Suck. *I want you to love me and accept me* *while I'm in it.* Those solutions and recommendations may be great ideas. But a **2** is not typically the most receptive state. Consider holding onto those ideas until later.

Imagine you're running late for work. You're stressed, anxious, stuck in traffic, and you know there's nothing to be done. You're going to be late. Now imagine a loved one says to you (while you're in a frazzled, tardy state): "Have you thought about leaving earlier?" Or, "You should go to bed earlier and stop looking at screens an hour before bed. Then this won't happen." "Stop stressing! It'll be fine."

Do you really think you'd be receptive? Probably not. *This* is a lot like *that.*

Some Supporters struggle with the idea of simply allowing someone to be depressed[24] or anxious or burnt out. You may even take it personally if your Sensitive loved one doesn't want your input. Supporters may think: "But don't you want to feel *better?!*"

I can only speak for myself when I say the following: No. I do not want to feel *better* right now.

I simply want space to feel exactly how I'm feeling without anyone trying to change me.

---

[24] Of course, there may be times we need an outsider to step in and help yank us out of the Suck. Continue conversations with your Sensitive loved one so you both can learn when that time is and isn't.

I think a tough thing for Supporters is that you may "come online" sooner to that fact that your loved one is struggling. You may see the signs well before they do, and they may not be ready to listen or do something about it.

It might help to write down your ideas and wait until we're in a more receptive frame of mind. And how about, just this once, you don't try to fix the situation? Consider removing the Fix-It Hat and instead offer the same TLC you would if your loved one had a belly ache or a head cold.

If you're not in the headspace to offer that TLC, perhaps you can simply give them space. Instead of trying to "fix" anything, just let them be right where they are.

Here's a little spot to write a few Supporter notes:

3

THE FUCK-ITS

(over it; irritated; 93% of everything sucks)

"Don't get me started."

"This is fucking stupid, and I feel sorry for all humans because we are sheeple. Just little ants in our little cars going to jobs we hate."

— JEN at a 3

*Dear Jen at a **3**:*

You're allowed to be angry. There are even ways to use anger for good. There are also ways to use it for bad, but they're generally frowned upon and tend to be a lot messier. And oftentimes illegal.

And it's totally okay if this section's tips and tricks annoy you. I've included some real-talk tough love, because you're strong enough to handle it.

No matter what, the fuck-its will pass. Oh, and stop furrowing your brow, silly. The Frownies patches can only work so hard.

The world doesn't stop for you.

Feeling pissy? Like everything is imploding on you or like life is pointless, or at the very least a waste of time?

Cool, cool. I feel you. Guess what? **The Earth keeps on turning.**

Your responsibilities still exist.

This is one of those annoying truths I'm regularly reminded of as a bonus parent to my partner's two kiddos. No matter how pissy or annoyed or anxious I am, I still must show up to sing Disney songs to the youngest one before bed. I still help pick out outfits, braid hair, and listen to the eldest talk about her newest favorite video game. And, no matter how shitty of a mood I'm in, I still hold the moral obligation to run around with T. rex arms when they initiate a T. rex galavant[25].

There's something to be said about resting and relaxing and allowing the feelings to exist. It's okay if you must lighten your workload or social commitments. But I've found that *I feel better about myself when I follow through on commitments*. This is annoying, and it's true.

Think about it. Let's say you flake on all the responsibilities because *HARUMPH*. The Brain Storm will pass, or certainly lessen. When it does — and if you've been hiding from life — you'll be left with a laundry list of past-due responsibilities paid forward from your Stormy Self.

This is okay, of course. Future You can likely pick up the slack from Present You. But, if you *keep* kicking the can on responsibilities, that's a big ol' bummer for Future You.

I used to be a flake. I dropped the ball on relationships and opportunities because I'd cancel or no-show last minute, blaming depression. It is true that leaving the house often felt impossible when in the Suck. But, truth be told, I had zero trust or accountability with myself. Zero discipline. I'd say yes to things I knew I didn't want to go to, panic the days leading up to it, and then simply *not show up*. I'd tailspin into a shame spiral after flaking, and

---

[25] We assume the body and arm position of a T. rex and run around the house. All other humans must follow. The dogs judge harshly.

beg for the person's forgiveness. After a few times, they normally stopped inviting me or stopped talking to me.

From experience, I now know that taking the next uncomfortable step and riding the momentum of that action helps me feel like a decent human being, if nothing else. Also, after the initial internal temper tantrum when someone (including myself) holds me accountable for a responsibility, I am sometimes even... in a better mood afterward. *What is this sorcery?*

I remember the first time my partner told me: "Life doesn't stop just because you're having a bad day." I got pissed off and simultaneously turned on by the rigorous truth of what he'd said. I don't have to fully disengage from everything just because I'm cranky. Life keeps going, and I can too. Even if I'm irked about it.

Stop flicking the brain bean.

It's easy for me to spin out when in a **3** headspace. Stories feed thoughts, which then seek out other evidence to feed the original stories. *What do I mean by a story?* These are the internal narratives that our sweet brains default to. Also called "limiting beliefs," they are storylines we've collected throughout our lives. As tiny humanoids, we may have heard variations of the stories from adults and adopted them as our own, or created the storylines in response to a painful experience.

Here's an example. In seventh grade, I tried out for the talent show and didn't make it[26], and thus decided it was because "I was a bad singer." I believed that story as a "fact" for over twenty years, to the point that my throat would close if I tried to sing in front of anyone. A few years ago, I worked with a vocal coach and realized I have a beautiful singing voice. I just had to rewrite that old story.

I am still rewriting the limiting belief that "I'm not cut out to be a parent." I thought I was too selfish and too unstable to raise children, which is one of the many reasons I never had any of my own. (That, and basic commitment issues. I can barely decide what I want to order for dinner without second-guessing my choice; I'm not really up for the permanent choice of creating spawn.)

Then, I fell in love with a man who has two kiddos, and I committed to bonus parenting.

When I get exhausted or cranky or have sensory overload, I want everyone to leave me alone and stop touching me. I just want to run away to the woods and live my best bog witch life with my dog, Floyd. My exhausted brain starts strengthening the story of "I'm not cut out to be a parent" by interpreting my cranky feelings as "evidence" to back up this storyline.

Oh, you want to be left alone rather than be fully present with the kids 24/7? Welp, Jen, that means you're

---

[26] Because we didn't bring the instrumental CD for *Backstreet Boys*.

not cut out to be a parent[27]. You should probably move away!

Suddenly I'm wrapped up in an alternate mental world where I feel *certain* that I should run away and *certain* that I'm not cut out for parenting, *when nothing has actually changed.* Rather than thinking: "Maybe I'm simply tired and this is a normal reaction for an Earth human..." I catastrophize and think of worst-case scenarios! I plan breakup conversations in my mind and feel the feelings associated with the grief that'd come from the breakup. Y'know, *the breakup that isn't actually happening.*

I'll lean into the pain of the limiting story, listen to only sad or angry songs, continue to seek out more evidence to back up the mean story, and dig my finger into the emotional bruise. My therapist calls this "mental masturbation[28]," because I'm just deedling the thoughts and stories and pain.

As my partner says: "Everything out here is the same. It's just fine. The only thing that's changed is your perspective." He's right. Just because I'm cranky or want to run away doesn't mean that life is any less awesome than it was last week when I was at a 7. It just means... I'm tired and cranky. The end.

---

[27] It turns out that most (or all?) parents get overwhelmed and want to be left alone. It's normal! Phew!

[28] I call it "mental edging," because there's never the release of an orgasm. Pedantic? Maybe. More accurate? Definitely.

So, what can we do to change our perspective?

Say the Limiting Story Train has already left the station and the thoughts keep coming even *after* we've recognized that we're caught in a story. We can simply start with the *awareness* that our current state is a perspective issue, and that reality is temporarily out of focus. **Recognizing the story while we're in it is a *huge win.***

This awareness helps pull us out of the narrative so we're no longer the main character moving through a scene with little awareness or choice. Instead, we become a witness, like an audience member in a movie theater. We can begin to see life a little more clearly from this view.

I use my feelings as a cue: "My reaction clearly doesn't match what's happening. I feel super panicked. My skin feels prickly. What thought or story is behind this?"

Once I'm able to put words to that thought or storyline, my next goal is to refuse to react to it. Experiencing the thoughts and feelings associated with an old story and *not reacting* is some hardcore, graduate-level work.

It's like if we only turned left our whole lives and suddenly learned that turning right was also an option. Muscle memory will have *everything in us pulling left* as we put extra effort into turning right. It takes practice!

Another approach I've found helpful for disengaging from a sticky thought is to tell myself the story of Jen from the point of view of an objective narrator.

Or, when it comes to the storyline about me sucking as a parent, I'll share honestly with another parent. I remember telling the kiddos' bio mom that I was struggling and feeling certain I wasn't meant to be a parent. I was terrified she'd judge and hate me. Instead, she was like: "Totally. This job is hard. I feel that way too sometimes!" And now we've become super close friends who can vent to each other without judgment. What a gift!

Any of these approaches removes me from the subconscious spinout and brings the thoughts into the light. Then I can watch them on the big movie screen of my mind while nibbling on etheric popcorn, drenched in galactic butter.

Don't be an ass hat.

Just because you feel like a bag of asses doesn't mean it's cool for you to treat those around you poorly. I know the temptation is there because you are hurting. And because people right now seem especially gross and annoying[29].

This doesn't mean you have to pretend everything is fine, hold it all in, or put on a fake smile. You can be honest about what you're experiencing *without* attempting to blame or spew your pain onto another.

I like giving my loved ones (or even people at work) a heads-up: "I'm in a cranky mood and it has nothing to do with you." I may also add: "I don't need it to be fixed. It'll pass in its own time. Thank you for your patience."

Or some fun humor, because that's who I am: "Please keep your arms and legs inside the vehicle to stay safe from the increased levels of sass."

Admittedly, this is a tricky balance for me because perfectionism and people-pleasing tendencies run deep. I'll recognize I'm in a pissy mood and then want to "save" everyone from how "awful" I am. *I don't want to hurt or burden anyone, so I'll just sit in my shit alone.* Or I'll pretend I'm fine, which I'm not nearly as good at as I think I am. People are way more intuitive than we give each

---

[29] Seriously. What's with all the mouth noises? And the *pen-clicking!*

other credit for. We can typically tell when something is off, even if we can't put our finger on what it is.

It's important to give yourself space to be exactly as you are, and I have faith that you can do it without being cruel to those around you. But even if you unleash your increased levels of sass? You have people in your life who love you, and **who will forgive even your snarkiest of days**.

I think the balance point here is: Don't actively try to hurt another just so you can feel momentarily better. Don't try to *hot potato* your Ouch to them. That just results in a big dose of shame once the Suck lifts. Plus, people have their own crap to deal with; they don't need yours, too.

If you do get reactive or become a spicy meatball? Take responsibility for your behavior, make amends, and move on. Try to be a little less outwardly spicy next time.

Oh! And taking responsibility is not: "I'm sorry if I hurt your feelings." Taking responsibility is owning up to a behavior: "I was super snippy with you. You didn't deserve that." When we cut through the noise with direct honesty, it often births the most amazing conversations.

Moving will not fix this.

Wherever you go, there you are. *Yep. That annoying saying again.* It's true, though. I used to think I was miserable because of the:

> WRONG RELATIONSHIP, WRONG
> JOB, WRONG MEAT SUIT,
> WRONG HAIRSTYLE, WRONG
> FOOD CHOICE, WRONG ERA.
>
> WRONG PLANET.

I'd point the finger externally, assuming my inside feelings were because of all these outside things.

When we make a drastic decision in this type of headspace and pull the plug on a relationship or job or whatever, we may feel relieved at first. *This relief can be confused as confirmation. That's not necessarily the case.*

I've found that I normally start romanticizing abrupt changes *when there are uncomfortable feelings I'm avoiding.* How many people do you know who get a haircut or tattoo after a breakup? Maybe it's to mark the start of a new chapter. Or *maybe* it's a distraction from the underlying feelings. It could be a bit of both. As my friend Hailey says: "Do I *really* want bangs or am I just sad?"

A little distraction is fine – and very human. Complete avoidance is where we get in trouble. If we don't learn to feel and process an ouchy emotional time, it *will* come back to be felt. And it'll bring its friends[30].

---

[30] They're often bigger and louder.

That temporary relief wears off. It always does.

Good thing, too. Because pain tends to bring delicious lessons[31]. Pain is an amazing teacher. A tough one. Strict. Unrelenting. And very, very effective.

I remember deciding that my depression was clearly because I lived in Kennesaw, Georgia, and had never traveled. *I'm obviously meant for grander places like Europe! That's where I'll find happiness!*

I went to England to stay with a delightful, supportive human for three weeks. We were going to travel to Ireland and other beautiful places. He had it all planned out.

I slept on the sofa most of the time, deeply depressed.

Wait, *what?* You mean, the depression followed me here? But I'm in a different time zone!

---

[31] I've heard that joy can bring wonderful lessons, too. I'm willing to believe that, though my experience thus far has been more of the... spiritual-elbow-to-the-face-to-get-my-attention kind of lessons.

This was an AHA! moment for me. I realized that moving or traveling or shaving my head or breaking up with people when I was in the Ouch — these were not answers. They offered temporary relief, but not a solution.

I've heard this from others, too. There are those who've followed the yearning to up and move and start over. At first, they felt great. But after a while, the same type of shit started happening in the new location that had previously occurred. Similar relationship dynamics, issues with work, health concerns, and so on.

Wherever they went, there they were.

Real talk: I find this to be superbly lame. To this day, running away is what I most yearn for when I'm struggling. I'll tell my partner: "I'm sad and annoyed and I want to run away to the woods and change my name to Towanda." And he's like: "So then you'll just be sad and alone... in the woods?" *Ugh!* Or he'll go: "Have fun. I'll see you when you get back." Which is also annoying because he's not at all reacting to my Towanda threat in the way I desire.

I've found the most powerful thing to do is feel – instead of run away from – the uncomfortable emotions. Have that conversation we've been avoiding. Get curious about why we behave the way we do. Try new behaviors.

Traveling is great, by the way. Same with haircuts and tattoos and ending shitty relationships. I'm not condoning staying put forever, growing a mullet out of laziness[32], or remaining in a toxic relationship. My point is to check in with your honest intention behind these decisions.

If you're trying to escape something, consider turning to face it head-on instead. At the very least, do a side-eye peek over your shoulder and *glare at it.* "I see you, thing I want to escape. **And I refuse to run away from you.**"

I'm pissed because...

One of my favorite things to do when in a **3** is to make a list of everything I'm pissed about and annoyed at, and what I want to do with that anger. I spew it all out in writing, with full permission to be petty. Then, I set it aside for Future Me to revisit. Or, if there's something kind (and legal) to do in the moment and I feel up to doing it, I will.

---

[32] I am, however, a fan of a mullet on purpose. A mindful mullet, if you will. Namaste, namullé.

Most of the time, the stuff I'm fuming about becomes a non-issue once I revisit the list a few days later. This also gives me insight into myself, what makes me tick, and what I care about. Looking at the list in hindsight, I almost always can see clear themes. The theme could be that I'm being nitpicky about my partner. If I dig a little deeper into that, I could discover that there's something I'm upset about that I haven't shared with him yet. So then very basic human things — like the sound of him breathing — infuriate me. But I'm not *actually* mad about the breathing. I'm mad about the thing I haven't discussed with him yet. The loud breathing is just easier and readily available for me to scowl at.

A next step with a list like this is to go through the "I'm pissed because" items and see *what I can change.* As in, are there any of these things I can *do* something about? Because really, I can either accept what's annoying me, or I can do something about it. These are the two options. Or I guess the third option is to sit and stew and sulk about it, but the sick sense of enjoyment that comes from wallowing in such a state gets old eventually.

Anger and passion are practically roommates. With practice and a wee bit of curiosity, we can learn to transmute anger into passionate or creative action.

What are you pissed about? And what can you do about it? Write it out, let it out on paper. Be judgmental and petty. If nothing else, this will stop the issues from bouncing around your head and will put them in a format you can address. For me, having an allowance for uninhibited sharing helps me quickly see the truth behind loud emotions. *Better out than in*[33].

Keep this list for Future You in a **6+** mindset to address.

Oh, and if you'd like some space to be unspiritual and vent with a trusted humanoid, the **+1** Supporter subsection "Permission to speak freely" (page 127) is all about that! Before you excitedly spew stored-up anger at your Supporter, though, make sure to set the stage first. And ask them if *they* have the space for a venting session.

Ignore the romance of what isn't.

It's tempting to sink into victimhood and this idea that other people have it better or easier than I do. But, trust me, everyone on some level experiences *the Suck*. Everyone gets belly aches and zits and has weird fears and heartbreak. Every human has boring days. All of them. Even Beyoncé. Although hers are probably catered.

Have you ever longingly spied on people's filtered posts on social media, using their apparent success and

---

[33] I learned that from my dad. He's normally talking about farts. It applies here, too.

happiness to *bully yourself*? I used to love comparing my sulky sadness to the Instagram page of a guy I once dated in high school, who now works in film and has a darling wife and children (all of whom have shampoo-commercial-gorgeous hair). I compared what I *interpreted* from those pictures to my reality: I was 30, living in my parents' basement, eating almond butter right out of the jar with a spoon I hadn't washed since my last almond butter date. I created the storyline that their life was so much better than mine. Based on one photograph. *Look at them; they're clearly perfect and worry-free!*

Years later, I reconnected with them and learned that there'd been health issues, job challenges, and more. None of that was visible in the adorable, smiling, freshly-shampooed photos. **We can never truly know what other people are going through.**

My partner once told me that my behind-the-scenes *is* my show because of the way I vulnerably share through my writing and videos. Being a very open person, I tend to expect everyone else to be the same, and assume that each online post (or in-person conversation) reveals their unfiltered reality. It rarely does.

Another way I romanticize what *isn't* is by focusing on what I don't have that I do want, and then pouting about it. *Oh, woe is me! I don't have a literary agent yet and I deserve one. I work sOoOoOo hard! This isn't fair!*

Admittedly, my **3** vibe is akin to Veruca Salt from *Willy Wonka & the Chocolate Factory*.

Or, I'll start viewing all my dreams and big goals as unattainable compared to where I am in life right now. While I logically recognize these are privileged stressors to have, that knowledge doesn't magically erase the "I don't care how, I want it now!" vibe. I normally just get angrier that there are so many people suffering in the world.

I've found that a good starting point when I'm in this cranky-pants mindset is simply *being willing to see the situation differently*. Even with an angry scowl, I can roll my eyes and say, "*Fine*. I am willing to see this differently."

Be *willing* to let go of what isn't. Be *willing* to let go of your idea of what others have that you don't. You don't know what their lives are like behind closed doors. You don't know the demons they fight.

Nothing good will come from beating yourself up over what you've yet to accomplish. You wouldn't do that to me, would you? Stop doing it to yourself. Be nice to my friend.

Take a breath, disengage, and stop creating dramatic stories about what you do and don't have versus what others do and don't have. It really is a pointless and wholly unhelpful activity to beat our Present Self up for not being our Future Self.

The comparison monster (I call him "Carl") may be tempting, but never yields positive results.

Scream and punch shit.

Sometimes, anger simply needs a form of expression. Maybe we have no idea what we're angry about, or maybe it's something we have zero control over. Perhaps we're just fucking pissed, man.

Being involved in martial arts has been amazing for me, because two times a week I get to safely beat the shit out of stuff without getting in trouble.

For my first couple years in sobriety, I used the *plastic baseball bat and pillow trick*. I'd buy kids' plastic baseball bats (in bulk because I'm strong and they break under the brute force of my power[34]), put a consenting pillow on the floor, and beat the shit out of it.

------

34 They're cheaply made.

I also discovered screaming. Deep, guttural, *Mortal Kombat* type of screaming. It's lovely. I highly recommend it. Your first attempt may be akin to the tiny "_{eeeep!}" of a mouse. That's okay. You'll get louder with practice.

I felt awkward the first few times I tried this. I was embarrassed, even though I was only in front of myself. But I kept on swinging that damn baseball bat, letting myself say whatever I needed to say. I'd do this in privacy, and I'd give myself permission to cuss people out or say that one thing I wish I'd said five years ago. Eventually, I'd tap into some primal, deep-rooted stuff. It felt incredibly freeing to give those old feelings a voice.

I learned that I had a lot of anger stored inside me. I needed a physical expression to get the anger out of me; journaling and talk therapy just weren't enough. Doing deep breathing to try and "calm" myself only further pissed me off.

Every few months, I'll feel a rage deep within my belly. When possible (e.g., not in the middle of a grocery store), I let it bubble up into a guttural scream. The pain and rage are *so intense* in that moment. So, I give them a healthy expression. Then, the feelings pass. **They always do.**

I've found that once I get the bulk of the fuming energy out, the root issue will become clear and easier to handle. Also, once I release the anger, I'll often just start laughing. *A lot.* It's like the laughter was hiding behind the rage.

Can't get alone time? Screaming into a pillow is a good way to quietly get the energy out so that no one calls the police. My screams are normally in the car[35], and I've yet to have anyone call the police on me.

Angry dancing is another fun approach. It's awkward at first, but feeling awkward is good. It means we're stepping out of our comfort zone.

If screaming and punching seem too expressive, give a proper *HARUMPH* floor stomp a try. Harness the energy of a petulant child: Scowl and growl and stomp the shit out of that floor. (I legit do this, like, once a day.)

Pause.

There's something magical about pausing when pissed off, taking three deep belly breaths, and then revisiting the situation. This is helpful if you're at work or another place where a loud scream may be generally frowned upon.

I'm not saying you should stuff down your anger. I'm saying it's okay to walk out of a room and take a breather. If the rage is still bubbling, I'll say: "I see you, anger. We'll talk later." (I *make sure* to check in with the anger later.)

Pausing has saved me and other people a lot of heartache. It's also saved me from arrest, if I'm honest.

---

[35] I once looked over in traffic and saw a woman primally screaming in her car. I was like, "Hell yeah! Let out that rage! You've got this!"

When we get anxious or irritated, our breathing becomes shallow. Our bodies move into fight or flight or freeze (or fawn) mode, which is an old primal reaction to protect us from imminent danger like bears and poisonous berries. Nowadays, most of us thankfully lack such physical danger. The "threats" are often emotional or mental instead, and not at all visible to outsiders.

We can say and do some gnarly shit to escape whatever we've deemed a threat.

Pausing, breathing, and taking a minute to cool down anchors us back into our bodies, back into reality.

Let's say we've held in a lot of anger throughout our lives and have yet to process it. When something pisses us off in the present moment, we are likely to tap into and feel a lot of that *old* anger as if it's happening *right now.*

So, you may currently feel super mad at someone or something. But it's quite possible that only a miniscule amount of that anger has anything to do with this current situation. The rest of it could come from the vat of old, stored emotions from past occurrences that merely *resemble* what you're experiencing right now.

Pausing (and breathing) allows us time to put Logic[36] to good use, to discover what's really going on, and find a healthy expression for whatever we're feeling.

---

[36] The noun, not the rapper. The rapper *Logic* is frequently put to good use. Have you heard his songs about anxiety and suicidality? Go listen. See? Even rich and famous people experience it.

Take a phoneless walk.

In a **3**, I may sit and spin out in my brain, feeling incapable of doing anything. I'll check my phone nonstop, hop on social media, or order stuff on Amazon that I'll inevitably forget I ordered and thus be surprised about upon its arrival. I go back and forth between busying myself in my phone, looking for relief through multiple text message threads, and sitting and staring blankly at the wall.

This is normally when my dog, Floyd, walks up to me and drops his slobbery, purple squeaky toy on my foot. Or, if I'm lying on the floor (I often am), he'll plop the toy on my face. Which I think means love.

I'll begrudgingly play with him at first. Sometimes, he'll even convince me to take him on a walk. This was hard the first few times, to get off my ass when stuck in the sticky Suck. But, I did it. Again, and again. It's since become easier.

Don't get me wrong; sometimes I tell him no, continue laying in my own filth, and then cry to *The Notebook*.

More and more frequently, though, I'm able to unplug from internal drama and my phone so I can play an overly dramatic game of tug of war or take Floyd on a walk.

I do this without my phone. (Audible gasp.) I challenge myself to be fully present with Floyd, with myself, and with nature. I focus on my breath, I try to find the colors of the rainbow in different items on my walk, and I do my best to put everything else out of my brain. Sometimes, I see cool things like little baby frogs or a squirmy inchworm. Or this one random discarded doll leg in our neighborhood cul-de-sac.

Other times, I see a dried-up earthworm and cry about how cruel the world is.

Either way, I'm walking. I'm moving.

Every so often, the original spinout continues for the duration of the walk, and that's okay too. Moving the body and getting in nature are two of the most helpful tips I can give on how to anchor back into the present moment and out of the inner workings of the mind. Even if it doesn't immediately help, at least we've done something active like a proper adult (if there is such a thing).

I dare you to go on a short walk without your phone. If that terrifies you, at least silence your phone and refuse to check it or use it for pictures on your walk. You don't have to post pics of cool shit and get "likes" to prove that it's cool. You can see beautiful things in nature and have them be, in that very moment, **just for you**.

Unplug. Chill out. Take a walk.

H.A.L.T.

I learned this annoyingly accurate acronym in a 12-step program. HALT stands for Hungry, Angry, Lonely, Tired.

When I'm panicky and can't put my finger on why, I'll check in to see if I'm:

- **Hungry** – This meat suit requires sustenance. When did I last eat? And was it nutritious? What about water?
- **Angry** – Am I resentful about something? Am I avoiding confrontation when there's something I'd benefit from sharing? Is Auntie PMS here for a brief, spicy visit?
- **Lonely** – I don't often get lonely (I tend to isolate and enjoy being alone), but I do recognize the basic human need for connection. When did I last leave the house? Have I talked with anyone on the phone lately? Do I simply need a hug from my partner?
- **Tired** – Do I need a nap? Do I need to take a break from work and watch a show? What kind of rest do I need: physical, mental, or emotional?

A note about being tired. I require a tremendous amount of sleep to operate this flesh vehicle without public meltdowns. My partner survives off 5-6 hours per night and a pot of coffee in the morning. And he's, like, *totally fine being alive.* I, on the other hand, require a solid 10-12 hours of sleep each night. I can handle 9 hours, but when I dip down into the 7-hour zone, I start to turn into a very scary, emotionally turbulent gremlin. Plus, I over-caffeinated myself in my twenties, so now even a sneeze of caffeine makes me feel like a panicky, methed-out squirrel.

WHATISTHEMEANING OFLIFEISITCHEESE?!

As such, *no coffee for Jen in the mornings.*

I share my sleep needs in case you also require lots of rest and naps. I used to feel embarrassed about how much sleep I needed. But maybe it's just part of being highly sensitive – I'm processing so much while awake that I need extra snoozes. So, I'll scream it from the rooftops: **I love a good nap.** Let me reset my brain and take a break from humaning for a bit, please and thank you very much.

In recovery, we tend to use HALT as a reminder to STOP before exploding on someone or doing something super drastic. Pause for a second and check in. More than likely, at least one of these letters applies to you. Eat a snack, take a nap, then revisit.

+1: Permission to speak freely.

*Your loved one's current state: **3 (The fuck-its)***

Oh hi there, Supporter. Your loved one may be a bit of a spicy meatball right now. I'm here to share an idea of how you can help. Here's a bit of background.

When I first got sober and entered the recovery world, I wrongly assumed that saying anything negative ever was *bad* and *wrong*. I thought I should only be grateful *always*, like some big Karma monster was keeping tabs on every negative or judgmental thought or word.

Perfectionism had found a new expression through recovery.

Let's say someone was cruel to me – an internet troll, for example. I'd force myself to immediately find compassion for them rather than allow myself space to be angry. *Oh, they must be going through a rough time.*

It's a great idea in theory; compassion is indeed the ultimate goal. But as it turns out, *the anger doesn't go anywhere when I avoid it.* It lingers in my body and grows until I want to unleash a decade's worth of anger if someone looks at me the wrong way or breathes too loudly.

This is where the power of venting comes into play. And this, my darling Supporter, is where we'd love your help. (If, and only if, you have the bandwidth for it, of course.)

Here's how it works. My Supporter and I agree ahead of time that **this is merely a venting session**. It's to let the steam out. I tell my trusted loved one: "I don't need a solution or a perspective shift. I just need space to be petty and unspiritual and pissed off." They tend to happily agree — because I help them with their venting sessions, too — and then I *let it all out*. I let myself cuss and say mean things about people. I let myself play the victim and whine and stomp.

The goal is an honest expression of the current pissy state. It deserves a voice, too.

The job of the **+1** Supporter is to recognize this session for what it is: a venting sesh. Don't apply meaning to what's said. Do your best to let it all go at the end. Flush it down the etheric toilet and shoot it into the starry sky.

My go-to tendency has been to try and bypass anger by seeking out compassion and understanding first. But then I battle what I feel inside (anger and annoyance) with how I'm acting (compassionate and understanding), and I exhaust myself. When I instead give myself permission to vent from a place of being totally petty, *I'm cutting through the noise.* I'm diving directly into the anger and giving it an expression.

Quite quickly, the anger dissipates. Once it does? Clarity arises in its place! It brings its friends understanding and compassion. And I normally realize that I also have a part in the situation that I'm so annoyed about.

And hey, maybe you both can take turns! It's freeing to let it all hang out, especially when you know it's a safe space. (It may take some time and repetition to grow a relationship into that safe space. This is totally normal.)

Go forth and be petty!

Anything else you'd like to add? Go for it:

4

SOMETHING'S NOT RIGHT

(out of sorts; outside of self)

"I don't know what's real and what's not."

"Why is this so hard? I feel like I do the work - consistently - and that the resistance I feel is far more powerful than what others go through. It shouldn't be this challenging just to be OKAY. Even basic things seem challenging and lifeless. I feel endlessly tired. No matter what I do, I always end up back here. Maybe this is my natural state?"

- JEN at a 4

*Dear Jen at a **4**:*

Oomph. The panicky discomfort of having zero grasp on reality is the Suck.

"Is this a pattern or is this something which only appears to be a pattern?"

"Am I reacting from old pain, or does my emotional reaction match what's currently happening?"

"Am I even working toward what I want in life?"

"What do I even want?!"

"Do I even like my job? My significant other? My friends?"

Take a deep breath, my sweet. You'll settle back into your senses soon enough. Wait until you're off the hamster wheel, then revisit these questions. This section will hopefully be some balm for your weary, uncertain soul.

What's "right" or "wrong"?

While in a **4**, I often immobilize myself with hyperanalysis around the "right" or "wrong" thing to do. This can be about big deal decisions, like job offers or traveling. It's more frequently about tiny things, like what socks to wear or what to eat for dinner. (I recognize that these are very privileged problems to have. That knowledge only adds to the overwhelm.)

Maybe my indecisiveness is due to being a Libra. Or perhaps my system is overloaded, making it hard to parse out the subtleties of intuition versus fear. It could also be that I apply tremendous pressure on myself and judge myself harshly for making mistakes or being less than perfect.

My partner made me this awesome cross stitch[37] of Bob Ross. It reminds me of something that I need tattooed directly onto my mind: *We don't make mistakes, just happy little accidents.*

---

[37] My partner is a bearded, heavily tattooed man who cross stitches. He's the actual best.

"Bobby R" (as I call him) sits on my altar space next to a chipped mini statue of Buddha and some stones and a sage bundle, because I'm a hippie in my heart and in my B.O. I was kneeling in front of the altar begging for a higher power to show me the difference between right and wrong. I opened my eyes, looked at the cross stitch, and started to imagine Bob Ross as the humanized version of my god[38].

Sometimes, my concept of a higher power is a hypervigilant micromanager who bullies and judges me. Like Bill Lumbergh from Office Space.

Hey, Jen. How's it going? We need to talk about your life performance. Mmkay?

I like Bob Ross better.

There I was, connecting with Bob Ross, when suddenly I heard in my head: "All colors are equal. All exist in

---

[38] If there is a god, I hope it's like Bob Ross. Or Morgan Freeman. Or just a giant tub of mayo floating through the ethers.

nature. Think of emotions as different hues for life's painting." He told me there was no right or wrong. No right or wrong way to feel. No right or wrong path to take, even.

Maybe I really was talking to Bobby R's spirit, or perhaps I needed a mask to stick on my internal wisdom so that I'd actually listen. I don't know, and it doesn't really matter.

Rather than stressing ourselves out about doing the "right" thing, maybe the right thing is to stop stressing out over silly shit. Take a breather outside. Set the issue aside and wait for clarity to come. Chasing clarity is like chasing bubbles. The more we frantically grasp, the more likely bubbles are to fly away or pop.

I've learned that the best bet for me is to stay still in my indecision, to chill out, and to wait for clarity to return. It's uncomfortable to sit still in indecision, but oh so helpful.

Other times, I check in with how serious the decision *really* is. If it has no real-world implications (such as which socks to wear), I'll challenge myself to *just quickly pick something*, damnit! Flail, if necessary.

If those approaches seem too abstract or challenging to apply right now, here's something that helps me. If a decision feels impossible, I'll keep searching until I find a completely different decision or action that feels doable hotwise[39]. *I can't decide which socks to wear. Okay, what about pants? Nope. Okay, I know for a fact I need to brush my teeth. Is that doable? Yes!*

The momentum helps my brain gears get moving. Then, I can revisit the original decision or thought after I've successfully figured out some easier ones.

This isn't all of you.

When I get in the **1-4** headspaces, it seems like I've always been there. I'll say stuff like: "Even when I was joyful, this was always lurking underneath." And, looking back through the foggy lens of these mindsets, that seems true. Whichever headspace number I'm experiencing tends to seem like the *only* truth. When at a **10**, I can easily discredit how I felt at a **1**, and vice versa.

---

[39] Once, when trying to say, "This tea is warm," my brain couldn't remember the word "warm" and said, "This tea is sippable hotwise." Now the whole family regularly says "_____-able hotwise." *Join us.*

When in a **4**, I assume all my amazing qualities cease to exist, that I must be awful and so much work to deal with.

But this current emotional state isn't the whole pizza. This is a tiny sliver of pizza, or a burnt piece of crust. It doesn't ruin the whole meal. We can even learn to appreciate the rest of the pizza that much more. While hyperfocused on one situation or state of mind, we may zoom in so far that it seems giant. When, in reality, it's a tiny blip – a crispy bit of cheese – compared to the rest of our experience pizza.

As a brilliant friend of mine says:

We are so much more than any one thing.

Let go of the why.

I can get so wrapped up in trying to figure out *why* I feel the way I do, because then I can at least have an illusion of control. I'll analyze the past few days and frantically try to apply linear reasoning to how I got to this emotional state. As if some specific blend of decisions is to blame for this **4** headspace, and it's all my fault.

There are times when an emotional trigger[40] is clear, and I can feel and verbalize the precise moment an old story got activated for me. I can interrupt and question my thoughts, disengaging from their roller coaster ride. I quickly return to reality, and I feel calm and grateful.

But there are *many* times when I have no idea why I feel the way I feel. I don't know what triggered the Ouch or what the lesson or deeper meaning may be. My tricks to disengage from spinning thoughts don't work, and everything I do seems to make the Ouch worse. Then, I start to panic at how out-of-control I am.

---

[40] An emotional trigger is something that causes us to feel a strong emotional reaction, often tied to past experiences. We may have a large reaction even if the current situation isn't actually a big deal.

Does it really matter *why* we're feeling this way? If we're in the mindset of indecision and panic, are we really in a place to solve anything right now?

In these instances, I'm learning to settle into a place of present-moment acceptance of how I feel rather than a panicked attempt to change or understand how I feel. In practice, that looks like me saying aloud to myself or a loved one: "I'm spinning out and can't grasp any one thought. It sucks." ← *That's acceptance, right there.*

I'm not fighting what is. I'm not spiritually bypassing myself by sneezing toxic positivity all over my thoughts. I'm learning to breathe, to physically feel the sensations in my body, to own how I feel, and to let go of this obsession around the intellectual "why?".

The clarity usually comes *after* the Suck has passed, not during it. Or maybe I won't know where the Suck came from or what the lesson was. Maybe it'll just be an ebb and flow without a say-so. That's okay. It annoys me to no end, but I can accept that the annoyance exists, too.

Some clarity comes as a profound realization. Other times it's a gentle shift. There's always progress, even if I'm not consciously able to label or define it.

It's okay to say *I don't know.* Or to say, *I feel lousy, and I'm annoyed that I feel lousy.* Shrug it off and get back to taking life one step at a time. Even if you feel uncomfortable, life continues happening. Accomplish one tiny task at a time and allow yourself space to feel exactly how you feel.

Is your brain overheating?

It's okay to watch Netflix and chill. It's okay to sleep or do mindless things. It doesn't make you lazy or a loser or frumpy or slumpy or any other things society may tell us.

Every now and then, the precious brain needs a chance to go offline so some necessary healing work can take place. It's that simple. This is especially true for people who are prone to burnout or ye olde depression. When the brain is tired, it's harder for us to keep up with our healthier coping skills. The well-worn grooves of old habits take less effort, so it makes sense that those behaviors feel easier when we're exhausted!

This is when we simplify our days and take the foot off the gas a bit. Obviously, we don't want to fall into the other end of the extreme and sulk in fart pajamas for countless days without talking to anyone (although very tempting). Find what's recharging for your sweet brain and do it.

It's taken consistent effort for me to tune into my true intentions behind my relaxation. I've learned that *rest* and *relaxation* are not synonymous with laziness or apathy. Have there been times when I binged shows to numb what I was feeling or avoid something I really needed to do? Yep.

Is it the end of the world? Nope. Is it at all helpful for me to beat myself up over it? Not a bit.

There are also times when I feel frazzled and overwhelmed, and putting a sentence together becomes a feat in and of itself. Even basic words are challenging.

This is a clear indicator that I truly need to unplug, power down, and allow myself space for *The Great Pottery Throwdown* or *The Great British Baking Show*[41] or whatever I fancy at that moment.

---

[41] I strongly prefer British reality shows to American ones. The American ones have so much drama and sass! I'd rather not be anxiously sweating about cupcake filling, thank you very much.

What are your signs of overheating? I start to get a burnout headache, I become irritable, and I feel restless as if my skin doesn't fit quite right. Tiny decisions can spark giant meltdowns. Issues that normally don't bother me can suddenly sprout into fire-breathing dragons. I also become very nitpicky about myself and others. These and other signs are my body telling me: "Hey Jen. Slow it down. Chill out. Watch a show or feel-good movie. Put together a puzzle."

Bottom line: The world isn't going to end if you sit and binge-watch *The Mentalist* or get sucked into your favorite mythology book. I think enjoying a good TV show or book is a lovely way to get a new perspective, spend quality time with my inner child, and stop thinking myself into a tizzy.

I also utilize meditation, coloring books, hot herbal tea, lying on the earth away from my phone, and taking Epsom salt baths as ways to recharge. Find what works for you, and then use it. Even if it seems annoying or your current mindset is all, "Nothing will ever work *ever*!"

That catastrophizing mindset very well may be an indicator that your sweet brain needs to cool down. So, cool it.

Pet a stapler.

This is a favorite trick of mine. It's a great way to get grounded back into physical reality. When I'm lost in thoughts, I'm not at all present. I move into autopilot brain mode and think about ALL THE THINGS rather than being where I am in the physical moment.

Maybe there's some underlying issue I'm avoiding, and that's why I'm in my thoughts and not in my body. Perhaps I'm worn out and burnt out and just need a nap and some homemade gluten-free cookies. When applicable, I blame it on Mercury retrograde or whatever the moon is doing.

No matter the assumed "why," the key is to anchor back into our bodies. Find an object. Pick it up. Feel its temperature, its texture, its weight. I mean, really put your focus into it. My lifer[42] Sandy and I like using a stapler for this exercise. I prefer a red Swingline[43]. It helps take the scattered focus of this:

I don't know what's what!

---

[42] We're friends for life. Hence, lifers. Sounds like a prison sentence, but life *can* feel that way sometimes.
[43] If you've seen *Office Space*, you know why.

To this:

I'm holding a red stapler. It's cold and heavy.

...it's my stapler.

The goal is to shift focus from abstract (thoughts) to concrete (something in physical form). This helps us to settle back into our bodies, because that's where our physical senses reside. Give it a try.

Call me, maybe.

It always helps to air things out, even if I don't know what's bothering me or why I feel frazzled. There's something magical about saying: "Hey, Friend. I feel ungrounded and weird, and I don't know what's going on. What's up with you?" Or perhaps it's a messier and more urgent: "The alarms are going off in my head. Help."

There truly is magic in sharing. It takes the power away from fear.

If you don't typically talk to people, I recommend adding that to your list of things to focus on in the future. Having a support group of trusted humanoids is paramount. If that's not something you have right now, or if the idea of talking to other people seems overwhelming, fret not. There's a bucketload of delightful therapists whose whole job is to listen to you when you need it. They've heard it all, and they'll gladly listen to you.

One thing to avoid is this odd tendency many of us have to call someone who will enable us, belittle us, further trigger us, or be an ass hat. I remember when I suddenly became aware of this behavior! I'd have an amazing thing happen – an opportunity or breakthrough – and there was one person I'd always call or text. Every single time, they were a fun sponge to my news. I'd leave the conversation feeling sad and deflated.

One day, I was about to call them when my brain chimed in: "Wait, don't you always feel lousy after talking to them?" *Well, yeah.* "So why not call someone else, then?" *Huh, I'd never considered that there was another option.*

I challenge you to interact with someone who genuinely cares about you and is kind. Or even that friend who only talks about cats[44].

---

[44] Hi, Kait! And Pixel and Digit and Lily and Monroe and Sapphire and the ever-present spirit of Princeton!

Another great trick is to reach out to someone you haven't spoken with in a while and ask how *they're* doing. Get outside of yourself, if only for a few moments. (Again, try to avoid people who tend toward emotional projectile vomiting. Stick to easy convos, if possible.)

Make a simple to-do list.

When feeling irritable, out of my body, or ungrounded, I'll often feel frozen when it comes to making decisions or moving forward in any way. In these instances, I love making a simple to-do list.

I simplify it down to the basics. Then, I pick two.

Easy breezy. By putting it on paper, it helps me stay accountable with myself and keep evidence of what I have accomplished, even if it has only been putting on pants and drinking a glass of water. If the list starts to overwhelm me, I remind myself I only need to pick one or two items. The rest are extra credit.

Oh! And if random side quests occur, I especially like adding those to the list just for the sheer joy of marking them off.

Forward momentum is forward momentum. One of my favorite sayings I've learned in recovery is "Move a muscle, change a thought." Sitting and stewing over something — especially if your brain feels like a herd of over-caffeinated squirrels — only makes things worse. Taking action steps, no matter how small, will help direct your energy outside of your mind.

And — let's be real — marking tasks off a to-do list is a glorious feeling.

If you're in a totally stuck place and need someone to *just tell you what to do,* the **+1** subsection "Just tell me what to do" (page 158) gives your Supporter permission to boss you around! Squee! (If you do seek their advice, I encourage you to, y'know, maybe actually listen to it. Ahem.)

Don't double-click that thought.

Being in a **4** headspace is often when limiting beliefs get louder and sink their claws in, making it challenging for me to discern what's real and what's not[45]. It takes everything in me not to go down a rabbit hole, searching for evidence to back up old, limiting beliefs, thus convincing myself that they *must* be true.

Here's an example. Let's say I don't hear from a friend one day. Logically, I recognize she could be busy. However, when in a **4**, my brain may unearth the story of "She's mad at me or doesn't like me anymore" and then create a whirlwind of emotions which correspond with this fabrication. It can even bring up the old, limiting story of "I'm not enough" or its opposite of "I'm too much." Getting wrapped up in that gunk sucks.

This is where meditation practice has helped me. When I recommend meditation to folks, I regularly hear the objection: "Oh I can't meditate because my thoughts never shut up." Your mind doesn't have to be quiet when meditating! The real skill is to have a noisy mind and learn to *witness* the thoughts rather than engage with them.

In many guided meditations, they mention watching thoughts as they pass by. Some say to put them on clouds, while others say to watch them as leaves floating away in a creek or river.

I've also heard to focus on the space in between thoughts to get into a meditative state.

---

[45] Callback to the **+1** "Real or not real" trick (page 65) from section **1** (**Meltdown**).

My personal favorite is to imagine a cannon and shove each thing I'm worried about, each story or thought, into the cannon, and then blast them far away[46].

Thoughts will come up in life, as will feelings. Old fears and stories are bound to pay a visit to say hi now and again. It can feel tempting — comfortable, even — to double-click a thought and fall into the rabbit hole of the lifelong tale of why that limiting story *must still be true.*

Avoid the temptation. Do what you can to focus elsewhere. It could be petting a stapler, listening to feel-good tunes, or even saying: "I see you, Thought." This helps us to separate ourselves from that Thought Folder rather than double-clicking and downloading all its contents.

We have the power to click or not click.

---

[46] I send them to a private beach. They deserve relaxation, too.

The more we choose *not* to engage with an old story, the less of a hold it has on us, and the easier it becomes to disengage from or ignore it in the future. The more we anchor into the present moment and into our current physical sensations, the more skilled we become at staying out of internal drama.

If the double-click already happened and the Thought's drama has its hooks in you, something as abstract as "just don't engage with it" may sound impossible. In these instances, I like to scream (aloud or in my head) "FAKE NEWS!" or "TABLOIDS!" at the thought. This seems to piss off my Intrusive Thought writers enough for them to quiet down. They're probably getting a talking-to by Management, who's sending them on unpaid leave to a beach for much-needed relaxation.

What's not working?

I despise the feeling of getting wrapped up inside my own head, unaware of what's right or wrong, what to do or what to avoid doing. There is so much information out there about how to handle tough emotional times, and oftentimes one bit of advice contradicts another. It can feel impossible to know the next right step.

I have two remedies for this.

The first is something my therapist told me. She recommended removing the "right" part of it and just taking a next step. ***Some* next step.** She explained that some form of clarity will come as we progress forward. A friend of mine calls it the "Pause and Pivot" move.

Take a step. Pause. Pivot. Take a step. Pause. Pivot. Take a step. While it may be slow progress, it's far better than sinking into the Quicksand of Despair.

Remember: *Move a muscle, change a thought.*

The second remedy is to **make a list of what's *not* working.** Or, perhaps, what *not* to do. Oftentimes, I have no idea the right way to handle a situation, or what I *want* to do. It's easier, though, to know the *wrong* thing or what

I *don't* want to do. This is data! Now, we have something to work with.

Here's an example of this in action:

> What isn't working:
>
> 1. When I don't leave the house for a while. 😭 — My shell hardens around me and leaving feels harder and harder. I can tell that staying inside for too long away from humanoids negatively impacts me.
>
> 2. Lack of physical activity. — I have all this angsty energy in me and it wants to move. When I'm inactive for too long, my bones and my mind ache.
>
> 3. Messy living space. — I can feel the panicky overwhelm when I walk into my office and it just makes me want to hide and sleep, thus further perpetuating #1 and #2.
>
> 4. All work no play. — With all the projects (the book, scripts, videos, etc.), I'm often in OUTPUT mode. And then I get angry and bored because my entire existence becomes about what I can DO for others.

Next, I can use this information to find the opposite of these items. This helps me compile a list of what I can do differently going forward, or what some healthy next steps may be.

What I'll [begrudgingly] try instead:

1. Leave the house two days per week. 😫 I added it to my Habit Tracker. I've been doing this for a few weeks and have noticed a drastic improvement in my mental health. Which is annoying, but good.

2. I don't wanna commit to a drastic increase in physical activity and then fail and be sad. Instead, I'm doing 3 minutes of stretching every day and taking the dogs on the longer walk. I'd also love to hike more.

3. I've asked for my mom and partner to help me do a deep clean of my office for my birthday! As for KEEPING it organized, I'm not there yet. One thing at a time.

4. Do something SILLY, fun, or restful. EVERY day. Put together a puzzle. Or play Nintendo, watch a show, take a nap. Refill my cup! This one is highest priority.

Now that I have the awareness of what isn't working and what could possibly work, it's up to me to take a tiny action step toward the latter.

So, what are a few things that you know *aren't* working right now?

And, what's their opposite?

Stop poking the booboo.

Are you feeling *or are you dwelling?* There's a difference between clearing out the old wound and sitting there poking at it just so it keeps hurting, like a cut inside your cheek that you keep chewing on.

It's important to feel our emotions, but sometimes I get carried away and lean too far into the pain. I'll listen to super sad music and think of horrible things in the world and do whatever I can to keep myself stuck in the stickiness of misery.

In those cases, it's time to **let that shit go**[47]. There are many ways to do this, and some days are easier than others. Physical movement is always helpful for me, no matter how impossible it may feel. Other times, I imagine putting all my issues into the palms of my cupped hands. Then, I'll physically fling my hands toward the sky and imagine all the issues flailing out to the stars. Or I'll shoot the issues via cannon to a faraway beach vacation.

Another go-to approach to "letting shit go" is to pray to god or love or the universe or to my higher self (whichever of those feels resonant on any given day). This doesn't have to be a bearded Zeus god or any specific entity. Just... anything outside of me. A friend of mine prays to the spirit

---

[47] If you're like, "How the heck do I do that?" Start by making the decision. Then, do what's right in front of you. Keep it simple. And *breathe.* The heavy energy and feelings will begin to shift. Promise.

of Alfred Hitchcock, because that works for him. Sometimes, I pray to Nature because it is intricate and beautiful and far more intuitive and intelligent than we'll ever understand. It's bigger than me, and so I talk to it from a spiritual standpoint via some form of prayer. I don't know why it works, just *that* it works.

To some, this may seem easy. Second nature. Others may deeply wish to avoid such a thing as talking to or even discussing a higher *something*. For those of you who are dead set against it, that's fine, too. Even accepting and admitting that you don't have control is helpful, without having to surrender control to a specific entity.

Heck, I used to pray to a painting on the wall. Even that helped because it stopped me from poking the booboo!

Breathe, and keep going. It's not up to you to solve all your problems and feel all your feelings alone. No one — not even Tony Robbins or Oprah — can do it alone.

So, relax your grip on the situation, un-scrunch your face, and give yourself space to move through this. *Because yes, you will move through this.*

♥ +1: Just tell me what to do.

Your loved one's current state: **4 (Something's not right)**

Supporter! Hiya! Your loved one is in a wonky, confusing headspace. And while much of the **+1** guidance is about Supporters learning to lovingly detach and encourage a Sensitive to find their autonomy, this subsection is all about the Supporter being the boss. Yay! (Also see "Lovingly boss them around" on page 304.)

I've found that the **4** headspace is a particularly good time for a Sensitive to ask for help. When I'm in a **4**, I'm stable enough to know I'm not about to blow up my relationships or melt down into existential despair. Plus, I really do want to take some form of action; I'm simply not in the mindset to know what that action "should be."

So, I reach out to my Supporter friends and say: "Hi. Do you have the capacity to boss me around and tell me what to do?" Normally they're like, "Hell yeah!"

Here's the fun part: I usually listen to them, and most of the time, they're right. Other times, their advice suddenly makes it clear what I *do not* want to do, which helps me discover what I *do* want to do. Hooray for clarity!

We share a mutual understanding that the other person has every right to completely ignore our advice. So, if your Sensitive loved one asks for your advice and then *completely ignores it*, I challenge you to laugh it off. When the pain of staying the same becomes greater than the pain of change, they'll become more willing to take your advice.

I've generally found that the best course of action is to have a good floor stomp and *then* do the thing the trusted Supporter recommended. What's really irritating is they're normally like: "You should rest and relax!" And I'm like, "**EW.**" And then begrudgingly listen to their guidance and realize they were spot-on.

You can add more Supporter notes here:

5

ROBOT MODE

(numb; indifferent)

"I mean... it's whatever."

"I don't even care enough
to write anything.
Maybe I'm doomed for
mediocrity."

- Jen at a 5

Dear Jen at a 5:

Thanks for bothering to read this section even though you currently have the motivation of a sleepy sloth. I know you struggle with robot mode because it's often more comfortable to feel pain than nothing at all.

It's okay to be in this hallway period where you're waiting for something — anything — to happen.

Rest. Do one little thing at a time. And, before you know it, you'll get some feelings back. Or maybe you'll learn to find comfort in the times of indifference! This section has some ideas of how to make this numb time a bit more tolerable. Hey; robots need love, too.

It's okay to feel okay.

General contentment has been a challenging emotional state for me. If I'm not feeling fantastic or like death, I interpret it as, *Hmm... Maybe something isn't right.*

PANIC ZONE

Feeling pain has often been interpreted as *doing hard work* and healing. On that same line of thought, feeling fantastic must mean I am doing a fantastic job and reaping the benefits of all Past Jen's hard work.

Getting caught in that mentality is dangerous for me. If I think that every warm and fuzzy feeling is a reward for past behavior, then I'm living in a world where I believe my joy and worth are solely dependent on how good of a job I'm doing. Then I get obsessive about moral dessert, doing good things only in the hope of good things happening to me.

It's much healthier and more enjoyable for me to believe in a less micromanaging, behavior-based world than that.

When life is calm and uneventful, I feel antsy and annoyed. I try to find something wrong merely to use my problem-solving skills on the problem *I've just created.*

Also, I've held onto a fear of mediocrity for most of my life. I thought that feeling bored meant I was boring and mediocre, which was obviously the worst thing ever. One of my favorite quotes is: "Life is what happens while we're making other plans." It's true. Life exists in the little details, in the in-betweens. In the traffic and the lazy sofa nights and waiting on the oven timer to beep. In the birds barfing up half-eaten worms to their cute little babies in their cute little nests.

If this calmness or boredom feels weird for you, almost like something is wrong, that's alright. It's alright to be in this space, to feel okay or "meh." **There is no need for chaos.**

Relax and take it easy. There is plenty more excitement to come. I promise.

It's okay to not feel okay.

It's okay for you to not be on your A-game. Part of proper self-care means giving ourselves permission to *not* feel okay, to merge with the sofa for a night, and to reach out and ask for help.

Maybe you just need to vent. Or stare at a wall and do absolutely nothing. *That's fine, too.*

I joke with my friends who also have ovaries that it's a good thing we have offset hormonal cycles. This way, we can take turns anchoring each other into reality and out of hormonal whirlwind stories.

If you feel outside of yourself or uninterested or robotic or whatever it is, *that is okay.*

Give yourself space to be right where you are. If that doesn't feel doable...

I give you permission to be less than perfect today.

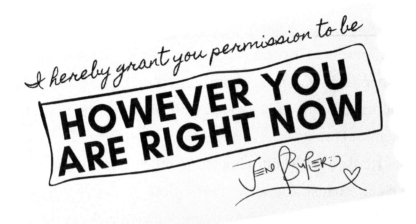

I hereby grant you permission to be HOWEVER YOU ARE RIGHT NOW — Jen By"er

Breathe, and try to enjoy this in-between time. If you're far away from enjoying it, sit with the in-between time.

With practice, maybe you can learn to *tolerate* it. That's a huge step in and of itself.

It's okay to not know how you feel.

I was talking with my partner about Valentine's Day. The cool chick in me wants to not care about Valentine's Day. And, on a logical level, I don't.

But, when people in the office get gifts, I find myself getting little flutters of excitement each time something is delivered, hoping that somehow, he was able to see through all my cool chick exterior and surprise me with something anyway.

Super healthy expectation, Jen.

I don't like these reactions or expectations. I want to 100% not care. I really do think the holiday is ridiculous and we should just eat chocolate and have the sex any day rather than on special occasions. But I guess I've been trained to want to be wooed with big romantic gestures. Thanks, Disney[48].

I talked with him about this much later in the year. Like... August. Because that's how I used to handle situations. I'd *not* handle them, hold everything in, and then fall into a deep depressive Valley every six months.

I tried to explain how I related to both sides of the argument, how confusing that was for my brain, and how I didn't know what I wanted. And he finally said: "You know it's okay if you don't know how you feel about something, right?"

Wait. What?! You mean *I don't have to know how I'm feeling all the time*?

You mean when someone asks: "How are you doing?" it's okay to say, "I'm not really sure"...?

Well that's a relief.

If the idea of defining how you feel right now is overwhelming, then don't define it. "I don't know" is a fine answer. "Fine" is a fine answer. Shrugging is a fine answer. It's all okay.

---

[48] Glass slippers are totally unrealistic when you take foot sweat and general chafing into account.

Learn to withstand the hallway.

Sometimes, life feels boring and bland. Sure, I can sit here and tell you there's always plenty to be grateful for and there are birds chirping, and you *should* be feeling giddy at the fact that you're conscious and alive and have opposable thumbs so you can open jars of nut butter.

But in real life, some days feel dull and boring and lame.

These are *hallway days*, when you've left one room and are walking toward the next one. It's the uneventful in-between space. I've had many hallway experiences where I've panicked into a tizzy, deciding that nothing good was ever bound to happen to me again.

I realize in hindsight that melting down into the middle of a hallway in no way helps me get closer to the next door. But I'm a beautiful, sensitive human. Meltdowns happen[49].

Keep moving.

The hallway won't last. We must traverse hallways to make it to the next room or building. Just keep doing the next right thing. Do the things you know you love even when you don't feel the love. Or just take care of little tasks right in front of you.

---

[49] I recently melted down over the impermanence of existence as it pertained to my loyal vacuum cleaner.

You'll make it to the next checkpoint soon. But first, you gotta keep moving. One wobbly, whiny, occasionally boring step at a time.

Just for today, don't shave your head.

There's also the temptation to do something extreme to feel something — anything — aside from boredom.

How I've handled hallway days in the past looked a little something like this:

1. Plan a full sleeve of tattoos.
2. Think of other countries to move to.
3. Want to shave my head. Again.

4. Find something wrong with a person or situation just to give myself an entitled sense of annoyance.

5. Random online shopping spree, which results in Future Jen's confusion as she receives multiple boxes with no recollection of what she bought.

EXHIBIT A:

Don't make drastic decisions just to feel something different than what you're feeling (or not feeling). That continues to perpetuate the same unhealthy cycle.

When *can* I make drastic decisions, Jen?! I'm not saying to avoid all leaps of faith or sudden changes. My challenge is to check in with *why* you want to make a drastic decision. When I make one, I also reflect on how I feel after the excitement and adrenaline settle. (Normally, I feel bummed and regretful. But not always!) I can use this insight next time I feel the same urge.

My goal is to be intentional about all decisions, even drastic ones (while also leaving space for occasional spontaneity).

I've discovered that a **5** isn't the best time for me to do a random shopping spree, pick a fight, or quit jobs. Historically, my "why" for taking a sudden, extreme action during robot mode was simply because I panicked during boredom. I craved a dump of feel-good brain chemicals.

But then, as Future Jen, I'd be paying off yet another ridiculous credit card bill and think: *Ugh, I really wish I'd stop buying shit and starting fights during robot mode.*

So, that's what I'm personally working on during the **5's.**

I'm learning to just... exist. I can add the items to my Amazon cart, and then *set the phone aside* before I order yet another inflatable costume.

So, consider breathing into and allowing the discomfort of boredom.

And maybe cushion in a little extra nap time.

It's okay to not feel much right now, or not to know how you're feeling. It's okay that not a lot is happening, or that you're in a hallway. Breathe into the exact space where you are now and set aside any major decisions (head shaving included) to be revisited in 48 hours. This 48-hour rule has saved me, my bank account, and the people in my life a whole lot of heartache.

I did buy a rideable inflatable T. rex, though. His name is Timothy. I have zero regrets. And I did shave my head. It was awesome, but the growing out period was awkward. I essentially looked like Ace Ventura for two years.

Alrighty then...

There's a saying in recovery called "Play the tape through." When we have a drastic decision we want to make, a relationship we want to end, a giant dinosaur figurine we want to buy for the lawn... we can "play the tape through" and consider the actual repercussions and impacts of the choice.

I know. Adulting can be so lame. But we can watch Rated R movies and adopt puppies. So... worth it?

It's time to reprogram autopilot.

It's great to witness myself on autopilot nowadays. I mean, I dislike not feeling present or fully "in control" of myself. I hate feeling bored or boring or in-between. But it's nice that the go-to autopilot for me has become taking care of responsibilities, while continuing to move toward healthier experiences and behaviors. I may roll my eyes about it and sigh and whine about adulting. But I find myself making it through normal life things without much conscious effort, thanks to all my past work.

Autopilot in the past was self-harm and self-hate and feeling terrified and untrusting of myself and others. I had to work extremely hard to aim myself toward anything resembling self-care. There was a time in my life when showering once in two weeks was worthy of celebration because I was so debilitated by depression.

Now I'm like: "This healthy living is kind of boring, and I'm annoyed that I have to shower and eat and other adulting responsibilities. But at least I'm relatively confident I won't yank my car off the road while driving."

My default settings have been and are continuing to be reprogrammed.

And that's what it's all about, isn't it? All this work around self-awareness, patterns, and making consciously loving decisions — with practice and repetition, the healthier behaviors start to become second nature.

If you're early in your rewriting journey, please know it won't always be this much work. It takes more effort on the front end – like a car accelerating to get on the interstate.

If you've been on this journey for a while and are feeling stale or unsure of your progress, take a moment to think of how you used to handle situations versus how you do now. Maybe it's how you handle angry people or confrontation, or how you make more loving choices with eating, or how you talk to and about yourself. Know that, at this moment, you are handling life better than you ever could have in the past. **Good freaking job.**

This, too.

Some days, I'm a pro at being mindful and fully present, able to enjoy the beauty of even the most mundane tasks.

Other days I want to light shit on fire and laugh as I watch it burn.

I remember the first time I used the *This, too* trick. I was working a job I despised but needed. I desperately wanted to hide under my desk, so I could still be on the clock (since I *was technically* in the office) but not have to interact with humans. I felt frantic, unfocused, and disconnected.

I tried something new when I recognized those feelings. I said, "This, too." As in... "Yes, uncomfortable feelings, you are also allowed."

That's been one of the most helpful additions to my recovery. When I notice that I'm fighting myself or my feelings or thoughts, a favorite cheat code is to say: "All thoughts are allowed. All feelings are allowed."

Normally, there's a wave of intense thoughts and feelings, followed by a *quiet mind*. Something about allowing the feelings and thoughts to be as they are rather than trying to fight them helps everything subside more quickly. It helps me to relax around the thoughts rather than get caught up in them. (I mean, telling myself *not* to think a thought is, in itself, thinking about that thought. So *that* approach is clearly a no-win situation.)

Most of us have felt pressured to be a certain kind of way in our life. To be happy, content, or stable. If we were too excited, we were told to chill out. If we were sad, we were told we were ungrateful or overreacting or that we should snap out of it. If we were angry or explosive, we were told to calm down. And likely, we're still repeating that same messaging to ourselves.

It's up to us to reparent ourselves.

It's up to me to give myself permission to be exactly as I am at any given moment. And to allow and witness, rather than fight, my thoughts.

Does this mean I sit and dwell in the Suck? I mean, *sometimes I'll for sure enjoy a mini pity-party*. But for the most part, I'll accept that I'm feeling how I'm feeling, and then I'll go about my day. Sometimes, I'm annoyed at having to go about said day. I accept and allow *that* feeling as well. I can do things while annoyed, or sad, or bored.

The world doesn't stop because I'm having a bad day. The world doesn't stop because I'm feeling robotic and uninspired. The world doesn't stop because I feel frantic or frazzled or uncertain or outside of my body. The planet just keeps on spinning and hurtling through space super fast, no matter what we do or how we feel.

It's okay to not be in a perfectly grateful mood all the time. It doesn't make us unspiritual or even ungrateful. It makes us *human*. And **all emotions are a part of human existence**.

The sooner we learn to accept that and ride (rather than fight) the inevitable waves, the easier this experience can become.

This, too.

There's this alleged thing called fun.

If you are feeling nothing or indifferent or a big bag of *whatever*, it's likely you need a solid dose of fun. Pointless fun. By pointless fun I mean you can't, like, *make money* from whatever fun thing you do. I used to do pointless fun paintings, but then people wanted to buy them. This was great at first. But then, the next time I'd do a pointless fun painting, I'd feel pressured to "do a good job." What started as free-flow fun became work.

Think of the stuff you loved as a kid. Is there a museum you can go to? An old favorite movie you've seen a thousand and one times? (I love *Men in Black*, *Benny & Joon*, *Twister*, *The Matrix*, and *Hunger Games*.) Can you put on some cozy jammies and sit and look at the stars? Do something to switch it up, without being super extreme. This refills the creative well and helps reignite a bit of passion for life. I call these "inner child dates," where I hang only with myself (or maybe with my dog) and do something merely for the sake of recharging fun.

INNER CHILD DATE IDEAS:

- Jigsaw puzzle
- Pick flowers
- Bake gluten-free cookies
- Watch a Disney movie
- Do sand art
- Doodle
- Coloring Book-opotamus
- Solo movie date
- Teach the dog a new trick
- Play with kinetic sand
- Swing on a swing set
- Paint for fun, not money
- Make paper airplanes
- Geocache
- Fancy bath with candles

Recently, I went to a local arcade and played games and laser tag. I went by myself and had an amazing time. I mean, I couldn't play laser tag alone. I played with a random dude and his two children, and my brain thought: "Maybe he's my future husband!" ... *Even though I love my partner, I never want to get married, and the dude was already married.* Intrusive thoughts so fun, aren't they?

If you are completely at a loss for what sounds fun or enjoyable, ask a Supporter to help come up with a few ideas. The +1 "Remind me what I like" subsection (page 183) focuses entirely on this! (I challenge you to ask a Supporter what they enjoy, too, and keep track of it yourself. These conversations tend to work best when they're reciprocal.)

Plus, there's a challenge on page 222 for Future You at a 7 to make a list of things you enjoy.

When I'm at a 5 and first start doing the fun thing, I'm typically super irked about it. But I keep doing the fun thing anyway, even if it doesn't feel fun. I logically know it's a thing I enjoy, so I trust that there's enjoyment hiding out somewhere... and it'll pop up when it's ready.

Sometimes, life is boring.

Roller coasters have ups and downs and twists and turns, and even flat parts where not a lot is happening. That's the time to recoup from the whiplash of the last freefall slope followed by the series of up-and-down bumps. We need the blank space, the time to breathe without much input or output.

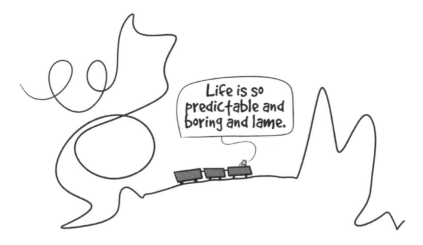

Blank spaces in life don't mean we are failing or that our dreams are any further away. There is so much happening beneath the surface that we cannot see. Our dreams and goals and successes are all on their way to us. Nothing positive comes from beating ourselves up about the "flat parts" of our life. In other sections, I talk about acceptance of the Ouch. Acceptance and allowance of squirmy impatience and boring whatever-ness *is just as important.*

If you're driving to the beach and pass a barren desert on the way, it doesn't make you any further away from the beach. Keep going!

Acceptance is very often what stands between me and peace. Accepting where I am in the moment is *not* giving up on my dreams or joy. Rather, I'm saying: "This is where I am right now. I see that. It is what it is." So today, I challenge you to accept the fact that life may currently feel boring or uneventful. I mean, you can sit and sulk about it. Or you can accept it. These are your options.

The slopes and twists and turns will start up again soon. For now, do something fun or silly or relaxing. Take care of mundane tasks around the house. Do what you can to let yourself cool down during this neutral space.

On some level, you're preparing for the next part of the ride. **Trust that.**

Find joy in the mundane.

After years of awareness and lots of practice, I still get irritated when I hit a **4-5** range and feel zapped and generally uninterested. But what I've repeatedly learned is that once I feel inspired again and am all GOGOGO, I'll be like: "Why didn't I enjoy that downtime more? I wish I had really let myself relax, rather than stress myself about all the other stuff I should be doing."

When I'm super tired or uninspired or am utterly indifferent, I'm learning to embrace those as part of the journey as well. I'm like: "Future Jen, I know you're going to be pushing the gas pedal all the way down and redlining, so I'm going to kindly enjoy this time of neutral nothingness on your behalf."

I still feel resistant to the mundane. But I also feel a sense of freedom, as if my own micromanaging tendencies are letting go of me, and I'm finally learning to truly relax.

♥ +1: Remind me what I like.

Your loved one's current state: **5 *(Robot mode)***

Greetings, Supporter! Your Sensitive loved one is in robot mode, which is when life feels bland, mediocre, or a bunch of *blah.* One of the above subsections, "There's this alleged thing called fun" (page 178), challenges the Sensitive to do something fun or enjoyable, *just because.*

When I'm in this mindset, I often have zero grasp on what I like doing. I once called my mom and asked her what I did for fun as a kid, because I honestly couldn't remember.

Here's where we may need to tag you in.

What does your loved one enjoy doing? What are some hobbies they enjoy, or a movie or show you know they like?

We're looking for easy, pointless fun sort of vibes.

So that way, when they're all: "I am so bored and I find joy in NOTHING! I don't know what to do for FUN." Tada! You can lovingly list off some of the items.

Hear me out. I know that it isn't someone else's responsibility to keep track of our every like and dislike.

But for me, when I'm in a robotic **5** and fully immersed in BOREDOM GOO, I tend to completely forget that fun exists and lose grasp on any idea of what I enjoy watching, eating, or doing.

When I'm at a **5** and ask my partner for a list of things I enjoy, he *always* has ideas. (Clarity is often easier for folks on the outside looking in.) I normally give him the stink eye the whole time he's listing ideas. But still, it's helpful. If nothing else, the conversation gives me some ideas and something to look forward to.

So, what does your Sensitive loved one enjoy? What do you think would be fun for them?

Here's a cute piece of paper for Supporter notes:

6
CAUTIOUSLY CONTENT

(hints of joy; awaiting inevitable letdown)

"What's the catch?"

"I feel good but am afraid to say I feel good. I'm afraid its vision is based on movement and suddenly the rug will be pulled out from underneath me. I have this on-edge feeling of waiting for some inevitable attack. Why can't I just enjoy contentment? And why am I feeling ashamed of how I acted during the 1-3 phase rather than enjoying how I feel now? Ugghhhh."

— JEN at a 6

*Dear Jen at a **6**:*

Congratulations on surviving the Suck. You know that angsty skepticism you feel? This section has some ideas on how to use that energy in a beneficial way. Don't forget to breathe, please. Yummy, deep, belly breaths.

Let go of past embarrassment.

Right. So. Let's say I've made it through a rough patch. Foods are starting to taste less bland. I'm feeling calmer, more aligned with real life, and less invested in fearful projections. Hooray.

Then, I remember back to when I was on the Struggle Bus and scrunch my face as my stomach drops with embarrassment and shame. Maybe I was dramatic or whiny during my stormy emotional time, or perhaps I took my pain out on someone else.

Guess what? That's, uh, *pretty normal.* We are human. That's not to say that I encourage you to be super dramatic, whiny, or take your stuff out on other people. I'm saying that if it happens, it's okay. When you revisit an icky behavior or situation after the Ouch lifts, take note of how it feels in hindsight. Plan to handle the next Ouch time differently.

Making amends is a magical thing.

Being able to laugh at ourselves is also a fun trick.

It's imperative to learn to embrace this imperfect humanness as a part of our experience. No matter how mindful we are, no matter how hard we try to emulate Gandhi, we are going to have times when we handle situations imperfectly.

And then... we learn from them. We make amends, we move on, **and we do better next time**.

Humaning is less of a graceful strut on a catwalk and more of a blindfolded stumble on a winding cobblestone street while wearing stilettos.

We're *all* stumbling, cute lil' potato chip.

Honor your past pain.

Emotions are all-encompassing when I'm in them. When in a **3**, it becomes clear to me that *this* must be the only reality. When I experience a little more peace – like a **6** – I can easily go back and disprove or even belittle what I previously experienced when feeling the Suck.

Pain is a valid experience, no matter how silly it may seem to outsiders or to you in hindsight. Honor how you felt, and please don't talk shit about Past You. *Be nice to my friend.*

After Brain Storms, I used to say to people in my life: "Sorry for being so freaking crazy." But then I realized that my saying that is talking poorly about myself, beating up on who I am and how I feel when in a stormy place. I'm not crazy when I'm at a **1, 2, 3,** or **11.** I'm just me, experiencing a different part of the emotional roller coaster of being a highly sensitive human, who is only now learning how to regulate her emotions and nervous system.

If we get scared while in freefall at one point of a roller coaster, there's no need to later be like: "Oh yeah that was so dumb that I got so scared." (We'd never tell someone else that they were dumb for being scared. Why do we say that to ourselves?) Just let it be. You were struggling, and now you're not. We can thank loved ones for their patience and support, and we can do so without belittling our past experience.

Feel the warm fuzzies.

I used to struggle to feel any sort of comfortable emotion, because I was just waiting for the other shoe to drop. It was almost more painful for me to experience a blip of joy and fall back into a painful place than it was to just remain in pain.

I kept myself in pain to protect myself from more pain. But that also prevented me from experiencing comfort!

It's okay to feel *good*. To feel a bit happy. To feel relief or a sliver of serenity. My goal is to get to a place of feeling serene more frequently for longer durations. This isn't to say I won't have low times or hyperactive high times. Through acceptance and building trust and integrity with myself, I am learning to feel a general *okayness* no matter my emotional state.

So, you're feeling warmer and fuzzier than you did in a **1-5** state. Great. This doesn't mean you're on your way to an inevitable doom or the rug is going to be pulled from underneath you.

Will the comfort last forever? *Nope.* Is that a reason to force discomfort sooner via panic? *Also nope.*

Keeping ourselves in pain or a sense of fight or flight to fend off the droppage of said other shoe is just an attempt to control the uncontrollable: *life.*

Do your best to enjoy where you are right now. **Future You can handle the rest.**

Just like anything else, this takes practice. I still struggle with blips of joy and find myself needing to do focused deep breaths so as not to panic during enjoyable moments! My nervous system needs some help getting accustomed to the comfortable times, too.

Prepare for maintenance!

Phew! The Brain Storm has passed. Before I forget the pain caused by this past Storm, I make sure to utilize that fresh rawness of emotion to prepare for the next one.

I used to stop myself from doing Brain Storm preparation because I had a way-too-literal interpretation of Law of Attraction literature. If you're not familiar, I'll save you from stumbling down that rabbit hole. The Law of Attraction is a philosophy that our thoughts and emotions are essentially magnets that attract more of the same. It's rooted in the idea that our mindset shapes our external experience.

And I get it, I do.

That's great for people who are, like, balanced in their mental states. But I was someone who fought myself to stay alive every day. Trying to force my uncontrollable thoughts and urges to transform into *only positive thoughts* resulted in a perpetual cycle of shame and misery.

I read that whatever we focus on grows, and that if I'm feeling "negative[50]" feelings, then I'll attract more negativity. I am a very literal person. So, I was all: *If I act as if I will never be sad again, then I'll never be sad again!*

If I plan for an emotional low point, does that make me more likely to attract said low point?

I'll just pretend emotional low points don't exist!

Then I'd ultimately spiral and sink into the Quicksand of Despair, totally unprepared, and feel like I just didn't *believe or try hard enough.* I'd tell myself that I must have manifested this pain by focusing on negativity in the past. *I'd shame myself for feeling sad, thinking it's some sort of repercussion of not being a strong enough manifestor.* **This thought process is damaging.**

I know there is truth to the concept that what we focus on grows. I also know that being avoidant about mental health is silly talk, and beating ourselves up for not feeling

---

[50] I'm not a fan of applying "positive" or "negative" to feelings. They simply exist. Some may be more comfortable than others, but I don't think it's fair to say one is "bad" while another is "good."

well is 0% helpful. Acting *as if* I didn't feel suicidal and depressed just made me feel more disconnected from self. It reminded me of being a kid, when adults told me I should be grateful and happy rather than so sad.

It's just like the obsession around self-love. If you can settle into a state of 100% authentic love for self and always experience every aspect of life through a lens of acceptance and gratitude, good for you. Enjoy being better than the rest of us. You're probably not even reading this because you've already ascended and reincarnated as the ideal lifeform of a bear who can nap a lot, never shave, and scare people for fun.

Jokes aside: If Law of Attraction is your jam and is helpful for you, go right on ahead. If it brings more stress than relief, on the other hand, maybe we can set it aside for a wee bit and focus on right-sizing our goals. Instead of self-love, we can first try to master self-tolerance. Instead of striving for 100% positive thoughts, maybe we can start by not blaming ourselves when shitty things happen.

If you had to live in an area that experienced hurricanes, what would you do? Would you adopt the *out of sight out of mind* mentality, only think positively, and just wing it if something happened? Or would you do what you could to plan better for the next potential storm?

It is *helpful*, not harmful, to share about our emotional Valleys and take note of what we've learned and what we can do to better support ourselves going forward. This doesn't mean we're attracting more negativity or depression. Our intention comes from a place of love and support and genuinely wanting to help ourselves. How can that be bad or negative? Life isn't that black and white. We're learning from our past and doing predictive maintenance. That is *positive*.

So, put on your glittery maintenance hat, and let's utilize the recentness of events to prep for the future.

Write down what you've learned.

Let's give Future You a hand. In hindsight, can you now look back at the rough patch with a clearer idea of what you needed? Or what, if anything, caused it? Would it have helped to relax more? To take a hot Epsom salt bath? Talk to a support group? Give yourself permission to be unspiritual and uninhibitedly vent to a Supporter? Eat less cheese? Eat *more* cheese?

Write this information down in the pages of this book or wherever works best for you. Just get it out of your brain and into the physical realm in a way that you can easily access in the future.

I go into more detail about curating this type of information in the **"How to make your own"** section at the end of the book. For now, here's a peek at a journal entry using *the hindsight insight approach* (page 327):

Hindsight insight example 1

Hindsight insight: This Brain Storm felt like pressure behind my chest and eyes and like I wanted to scream at everyone, but also wanted a damn hug. I was like, "GO AWAY COME BACK GO AWAY COME BACK."

What I needed: What I really needed was someone to tell me it's okay to be pissed off, rather than trying to fix me. Everyone kept trying to get me to focus on the positive. I logically understand the positive, people! But there's also a lot of pain in the world. Sadness belongs! Anger belongs!

What emotional state I was in: I was too overwhelmed to know exactly which emotional state I was in. But now, in hindsight, I think I was in a 2 (barely hanging on) to 3 (the fuck-its) range.

What to do next time: Next time, I'll make sure to tell myself, "Jen. It's okay to be pissed off." And if anyone asks how they can help, I'll tell them that's what I most need: permission to be exactly as I am at the moment. They can shove their toxic positivity right up their smiling butts.

Action step to take now: Now that I have a bit more insight into what a **2** and a **3** feel like to me, I'll add that to the empty bullet points in the TOC of this book. That'll help me more quickly navigate to **2** and **3** in the future when I need help pinpointing how I feel.

Also, I think I'll kindly tell my loved ones that I don't need reminders of positive stuff. I need to know that I'm loved when I'm cranky, too.

I highly recommend sharing this information with a Supporter, a therapist, or similar. And certainly, hold onto it for your Future Self.

A helpful note before sharing with a Supporter: *Ask your Supporter if they're in the mindset to hear about your breakthroughs.* This is a kind and loving thing to do! Without this check-in question, I assume everyone will drop everything they're doing and eagerly listen to all my self-realizations with bated breath. *Meanwhile, it's 1AM, my partner must wake up in five hours, and he's barely keeping his eyes open.*

Come up with a code word.

"The alarms are going off in my head."
"I'm really struggling."
"I'm spiraling."
"I'm tired of being alive."

These are the phrases I now use when I'm riding the Struggle Bus, in a depressive episode, or hearing whispers (or off-key screams) of suicidal ideations. The people close to me know the importance of these code words, and they know how to best show up for me when I get to those mindsets. How do they know? Because of this magical thing called communication.

After emerging from Valleys, once I make it to a solid **6**, I communicate with my support system and let them know what I learned *and what I need* during future Valleys. I answer questions, make amends if needed, and then we move forward a little more prepared and aligned.

My partner knows that "I'm feeling cranky and whiny" or "I'm super sad today" is one thing. That, for me, means I'm experiencing the normal discomfort that comes with being human, and it will all be fine soon.

When I use any of my code words and phrases, though, he knows that I'm sinking a bit too low or flying a bit too high. It's time for him to step in and help if he can. We also work together to get clear on what "help" looks like when I use one of the code phrases.

People want to be helpful. And, at a deep core level, we want to be helped when we are in a rough place. Everyone has different interpretations about words and phrases. You saying, "I'm struggling today..." could be interpreted as a not-a-big-deal thing to a friend, where in your mind it means: "Holy shit! I'm drowning! Please help!"

Of course, the ultimate goal is to be able to clearly express needs *in the moment*. I'm thankfully now at a place in my romantic relationship where, even at a **1** or **2**, I can articulate: "I feel like I'm outside of my body. I need to cry, but I don't know why. Will you please hug me or snuggle me and help me talk?"

Years ago, I'd have felt way too embarrassed or scared to say something that vulnerable. Trying to express my needs while in the Ouch would've yielded a panic attack.

Now, through building trust and communicating regularly (with myself and with my partner), we've learned how to best show up for one another.

Code words are a great place to start. *And, let me be very clear, code words should be used sparingly and only when it's a true red alert crisis.*

Communication is key. Other folks can't read your mind. *Help bridge the communication gap.* Use your current **6** mindset to your advantage. Have conversations with those close to you so they know how you experience life and how they can best help. Help them help you! Also, add the code words to sections **1** (page 41) and **2** (page 71), so that they're easy for you to access when struggling.

Oh, and if you try to avoid this exercise or hoard your code words like Gollum with the ring, I'm one step ahead of you. The **+1** subsection (page 210) gives your Supporter the task of coming up with code words, too. *Ha! I win!*

Yes, you will feel like shit again.

Life has ups and downs. It just does. The best way I've found to be okay with this fact is the mystical concept of *acceptance*. EWGROSSBARF, I know.

Acceptance allows me to be *sort of* happy, even when I feel super down and out. It kind of blew my mind that I could feel sad *and* okay at the same time. Acceptance also helps me stay humble when I start to feel on top of the world, because I know that this, too, is impermanent.

I used to feel panicky once I emerged from an emotional Valley and started to feel okay. I'd try to do everything I could to ensure I'd *never feel that sad ever again*!

I threw myself into unhealthy levels of self-care (yes, it's a thing – anything taken to an obsessive extreme can become harmful). I focused on showing up as my "best self" *rather than authentic self* to recovery meetings and in conversations with friends. I'd try to be positive and profound rather than honest and real. People thanked me for being so inspirational. Meanwhile, behind the smile, I felt like I was screaming inside, and no one was listening.

But I wasn't screaming. I was pretending.

I was doing whatever I could to try and control the whole life experience so I'd only manifest happiness and people were *only* impressed by me.

But guess what? Sadness isn't bad. Anger isn't bad. They just... *exist*. They are experiences. Bumps in the road, detours, or perhaps long stretches of desert which seem like they'll never end. In fact, I've found that uncomfortable emotions often yield the most scrumptious realizations and clarity. That's their gift to us.

The boring or bumpy parts of a road trip are what ultimately lead us to the fun checkpoints, landmarks, and destinations.

So, settle into your present moment. Allow yourself to breathe a little easier now that you're out of the Suck. Try to recognize that this is simply another part of the road trip. This scenery will also eventually pass. And the more we learn to accept this fact, the easier the *down* times become, and the less attached we become to the up times.

Learn your cycles.

Did you know it's common for people to struggle around the same time each year? It's different for each person. I mean, SAD (Seasonal Affective Disorder) is a thing that impacts lots of people where they're legitimately depressed during certain seasons. Maybe that's also part of your cycle, but I'm more so referring to specific weeks or months out of the year.

September used to be a really challenging month for me. March was, too.

Maybe it's astrology (silly Mercury in the microwave again), or maybe it's because of past traumas and the emotional memory being reactivated in some way when the anniversary comes around.

There's no way to know exactly why we feel the way we feel in any situation. Even the most educated, well-versed, self-aware person won't understand every intricacy of their emotional landscape.

But... we can get curious, and **we can begin to learn**.

I remember when I first noticed this cycle for myself. I looked back and saw a clear theme: I historically ended relationships, quit jobs, or got sick or depressed in March and September! Having the awareness of this cycle was a helpful step, because I learned to have compassion for and be gentler with myself during those months.

I didn't want that to be my forever, though. September is when Fall begins, and *Fall is my love language.* I don't want to be so depressed that I can't get out of bed to step on crunchy leaves. So again, I got curious: *It seems that this annual Ouch is a cycle of mine.* **Now what?**

Upon exploration, I remembered that when I was 19, I'd had a horrible car accident at the beginning of September. Afterward, my job was hard on me because my sales were down. The CEO's wife accidentally copied me on an email where she called me a "laundry list full of excuses" because I asked for a day off to rest. I had never really processed through how much that sucked.

As for the cyclical March struggle: I had attempted suicide when I was 22, in early March. For obvious reasons, that March was a pretty lame one. Mostly because the psych ward's food was *gross.* And they didn't trust me with a pen, so I had to journal with a blue crayon.

Through therapy, anger releases, and a variety of healing modalities, I finally processed through the bullshit I'd held in for decades. Now, September and I are besties.

March has again become the month where I excitedly wait for snow, rather than fending off confusing depressive symptoms with no apparent cause. (I live in Georgia, so our version of snow is essentially dirt with a handful of dandruff flakes. I still get amped and make snow/dirt creatures, though.)

There is no overnight fix. We start with curiosity about our behavioral cycles, which invites awareness to the party. Then, we can use the data we've uncovered to find a wee bit of self-compassion. From that place, we can move forward toward rewriting, releasing, and healing. Or, if you'd rather, you can accept that some days, weeks, or months simply are harder than others. That's okay, too.

Here's another example of an emotional cycle. Every month, my uterus gets mad at me for refusing to procreate, rips down the wallpaper she spent all month decorating, and shoves it out of my crotch hole. Even though this has happened every month for almost three decades of my life, I still am like: "WHY DO I FEEL SO CRAZY?!"

And then I bleed and am like, "Oh. Right. This again."

So now, I have an app where I track my emotional state, my energy level, and how focused or social I feel (or don't feel) on louder days of my cycle. After having the app for a handful of years, I'm able to reference past notes and go: "Oh. Today is day 18 of my cycle. The last ten months, I logged that I felt this exact same way on day 18. So, this is normal for me. Nothing to be alarmed about. Hormones be hormoning."

Even for those without an obvious monthly cycle, there are apps to keep track of mood, sleep, what you eat and drink, and so on. If that's too overwhelming, then having a general curiosity and awareness is a good place to start.

What are your cycles? Historically, is there a theme of when the Suck hits?

Note: Your cycles may not always be complementary with your Supporter's cycles. I'd say about 90% of the time, my partner's and my emotional cycles play nicely together. Either we're both in a solid, grounded place, or one of us is struggling while the other one is supporting.

10% of the time, though, our cycles don't play nicely together. Neither of us has the capacity to show up as a Supporter for the other. This is totally normal, and totally human. What we've started to implement that helps is: "How about we both simply allow each other to be in a shitty mood?" Or, if both of our internal batteries are *really* depleted, we lovingly hide in opposite sides of the house to do our own solo-recharge time.

It's helpful to discover what's hormonal, what's seasonal, or what has to do with anniversaries of traumas or rough times in the past.

The more you learn about yourself, the easier it will be to shift into healthier habits and learn how to process life with less resistance and less pain. At the very least, you can gain an understanding of your cycles. What a lovely breakthrough that will be!

Relax your focus.

This subsection is for my fellow hypervigilant people who like to do things to the extreme. *A+++!* When I first started exploring my mental and emotional landscape, my eagerness to learn regularly slipped and tumbled into the territory of *trying to control myself* rather than help myself.

This is a reminder for me, and perhaps it will be helpful for you:

> JEN: LEARNiNg youR cyclES ANd pAttERNS is to hElp youRSELf, NOt miCROMANAgE youRSELf. This isN't AN OVERNight "fix." It's AN ONgOiNg EXpERiMENt!
>
> RELAX YOUR FOCUS.

I can start fixating too much on tracking every little thing every day, applying linear reasoning to the unpredictably swirly shitshow of life. Like: "Oh I'm probably depressed because I ate almonds yesterday and I once read that almonds were bad, so I shall never eat almonds again!" When I get caught up in that hypervigilant mindset, I need to soften and relax my focus.

Here's what I mean by *relaxing my focus*. Imagine I'm scouring a *Where's Waldo* book or trying to find a single puzzle piece in a box of 500. When I hyperfocus and try *really hard* to find Waldo or the puzzle piece, I simply cannot. Then, I'll hand the *Where's Waldo* book to my partner and in 13 seconds he's like: "Waldo's right here."

I express my gratitude with something super sweet like: "WHAT?! SCREW YOU, MAN! WALDO WASN'T THERE BEFORE!"

He explains that I simply need to relax my eyes rather than trying so hard. (Cue eye roll.)

But then, I experienced that relaxed focus. I was desperately searching for a puzzle piece that apparently didn't want to be found, when I started thinking about a movie I'd just watched. I visualized the movie in my head, stopped paying such close attention to the puzzle piece search and rescue, and BOOM! I found the puzzle piece!

So, while the hypervigilance may *seem* like I'm "finding answers," I've learned that I don't have to take inventory of every thought, every hiccup, or every anxiety. Instead, I remain willing to do my best each day, recognizing that my best one day may be very different from my best another day. And I'm learning to be genuinely okay with that fact.

From that softened focus and relaxed allowance, the behavioral themes become clear to me seemingly out of nowhere, without me having to hardcore search or analyze!

I'll be walking the dog, showering, editing a video, or vacuuming, and I'll suddenly have an out-of-nowhere *AHA!* moment.

Let (or make) yourself rest.

Just because you're feeling more comfortable doesn't mean you should sprint around like an over-caffeinated squirrel and try to get ALL THE THINGS done to make up for lost time. This just continues the cycle of hardcore ups followed by hardcore downs. It's like a pendulum. The harder it swings one way, the further it'll swing the other.

It's okay to follow inspiration and motivation; just do so within reason. Maybe even take 30 seconds to move in hyper-slow motion. Just for funsies. **Funsies are allowed – encouraged, even.**

Continue the self-care recharge work. I must schedule my rest and relaxation time when I'm in a **6+** place. I often look at rest as a necessity to address burnout rather than an essential proactive self-care measure. (I admittedly treat self-care as a checkmark thing rather than something enjoyable, which isn't the best relationship. But, hey. It's just where I am at the time of writing this book.)

To prevent burnout, make sure you pull back on the reins a bit. Take some cooldown time. Read a book. Meditate. Sit in nature. Do a puzzle and don't try so hard to find that one sneaky piece. Walk the dog without your phone. Or walk the cat, if that's your thing. Watch a feel-good movie.

While I'm all about honoring our natural cycles and following inspiration when it arrives, I also have learned that for me — and others who tend to go hard and fast in life — it's imperative to chill out and relax. This is especially important for those of us who are hypersensitive. We are constantly receiving sensory input from the world around us, much of which we are not consciously aware of.

Downtime is essential. If it feels uncomfortable at first, that's normal. Keep practicing. It'll get easier.

+1: Come up with a code word.

Your loved one's current state: **6 (Cautiously content)**

Salutations, Supporter! Your loved one is feeling cautiously content. Now, let's be kind to Future You, yeah?

See – there can be a kind of "boy who cried wolf" vibe when in a relationship with a highly sensitive person who struggles with emotional regulation. My partner's confusion was: "When are you feeling the really big feelings and handling it, versus when are you out of control and genuinely struggling?" When out of the Suck, we worked together to come up with a code word or phrase. "The alarms are going off" means: "**RED ALERT**. I'm not okay. I need help NOW."

A code word can help you, as the Supporter, decipher what your loved one's internal world is like. My friend says to her husband who struggles with volume control: "I can't know what I don't know. You need to tell me what's going on." And, when we're past the point of being able to verbalize what we're experiencing, a code word or phrase can certainly help cut through the confusion. Here are some examples of code words (or, more accurately, code *phrases*) that I and my close friends use:

"The alarms are going off in my head."

"I'm really struggling."

"I'm spiraling."

"I'm tired of being alive."

This approach also helps your loved one begin to regulate their emotional state by learning what is and is not a red alert emergency. For people whose emotional state often feels like "AAAHHHH!" — this is a big step!

As for how this helps you as a Supporter: The more you work together to learn what a true crisis looks like (and doesn't look like), you'll know when your loved one genuinely needs help. And, together, you can learn what that "help" may look like in practice. This can free up a lot of mental and emotional space for you.

These code words mean: "Stop what you're doing. I'm drowning. Help me."

So, of course, they should be used sparingly and only when nearing or in a true crisis.

This exercise helps build communication and trust between a Sensitive and Supporter. In my experience, the code words are especially helpful for people who tend to implode and hide when they're struggling. While reaching out and explaining feelings may feel impossible to them, texting a simple code word or phrase is much easier.

Please also come up with your own code word or phrase. This could mean: "I cannot show up for you right now because I myself am totally depleted and struggling." You're allowed to have red alert moments, too!

Here's where you can add Supporter notes:

THE SUN IS SHINING

(calm; colors look brighter; optimism has returned)

"Oh yeah. I remember now: Life can be good."

"I'm really glad I didn't blow up my life and end all relationships when I was on the Struggle Bus. I can see everything clearly now! Life isn't perfect, but maybe I do have a purpose and maybe I can belong here. I kind of want to go back and delete what I wrote from the 1-3 headspace because now I have perspective! But I won't. Just in case."

— Jen at a 7

Dear Jen at a 7:

The sun is out, the birds are chirping, and you're starting to see a twinkle in your own eye again. Rock on! I give you permission to enjoy the sunshine. It's also time to do some proper maintenance and recharging work, because you finally have the energy and ability to do so.

This section shares some ideas on how to appreciate the 7 while also being kind to Future You! She deserves it.

Let yourself enjoy this.

Okay, "enjoy" may admittedly be too strong of a word for how I experience life, even during a 7. I do have moments of *bird barf glee* and delight and some longer spans of this kind of boring thing called "contentment." Enjoyment is a little more challenging for me. I have no problem bringing fun and humor and enjoyment to other people, I know that much. But when it comes down to me experiencing a body sensation of "joy," that's less common.

I normally discover I've been enjoying myself *in hindsight*. An intrusive thought grabs my attention with its over-the-top drama and morbidity. I'll feel my body and emotions constrict around the thought. That's when I smash the pause button and go: "Wait a darn second. What was just happening? Right before this thought?"

Through this hindsight, I discover that I had just been feeling some sort of fluffy joy. Then my subconscious apparently panicked: "OH NO THAT CAN'T BE RIGHT. BRING IN THE MORBID THOUGHTS!"

Having this awareness is super helpful. I'm catching the moments of delight sooner. The challenge for me is to mindfully relax my muscles and breathe into the moments of joy. Really anchor into them and try to catch joy sooner and sooner.

I've started even taking "mental snapshots" of delightful moments. Two recent examples: my 46-year-old partner playfully kicking and flailing under the covers like a toddler, and my puppy's reaction after she tasted peanut butter the first time (she was AMPED!).

In each of these moments, I laughed and felt a swelling of what I think is enjoyment. Upon noticing the joy, I immediately took a deep breath and imagined taking a mental photo of the experience.

Another favorite approach for when intrusive thoughts try to *shock block* my delight is to say "FAKE NEWS" or "TABLOIDS" aloud or in my head. Then, I find the pleasant thing I was previously thinking about or feeling and breathe back into it.

Maybe you're more skilled at feeling joy than I am. Hopefully, it doesn't send your body into fight or flight or make your muscles tense and jaw clench. Either way, let's let out a yummy sigh of relief that we survived all the stormy days up until this point.

I challenge you to focus on your physical senses. Take lots of deep breaths and pay close attention to the little details of the moment. Relax your muscles and stop furrowing your brow. **You're allowed to enjoy this.**

Remember the Ouch.

I was the most motivated to work on this book when I was struggling through a **1-3** headspace. Desperation is an excellent motivator. *I wish this book existed to help me; I'm going to write it, so it exists for others.* Then, in the **4-6** region, I'd feel mostly complacent and indifferent, and would rarely write. Once I made it to the higher numbers,

I'd want to go back through and delete everything I had previously written when in the **1-3** range so I could shit rainbows and optimism all over the pages instead.

I remember more than once feeling like I'd "figured it out" when in a **7** headspace. I said to a friend: "I feel like all those people who say 'suicide is selfish' are right. It is, by its very nature, self-absorption." (Cue a fan blowing my hair in slow motion as I walk away from an explosion and *never look back*.)

"Okay," he said. "But you *know* what it's like to be held captive by it."

OOMPH. That brought me back to Earth.

Yes, I've done a lot of healing work. Yes, I will continue to do so. And yeah, I am generally okay now in life, experiencing mostly **4-7's**. But, no matter how many realizations I have or how well I can regulate emotions, *this doesn't erase what I've experienced in the past*. Nor does it invalidate any future Ouch I may experience, or any pain or struggle *you* may experience.

I need to remember where I came from, and it can be easy to forget. Humans are adaptable creatures, and we have great built-in forgetters. I can't count the number of times I went back to exes because I'd totally forgotten how awful the relationship had been. (I was quickly reminded.)

Here's the point: It's easy to forget just how shitty things were. And, while we certainly don't need to dwell on past misery, it's also important to remember its existence and to honor our Past Selves. I think it's humbling to remember how hard life feels when we're in the Ouch. It helps me appreciate the 7's that much more.

Don't be a Stage 5 Clinger to joy.

Getting to a place of relief after a rough patch feels freeing and glorious indeed. This is often when my hypervigilance and control tendencies pop up, thinking I can direct life to make sure I always and forever stay 7+.

Any attempt to control my external world obviously fails. In fact, it ends up making me feel further away from myself, like I'm ousting the messier pieces of who I am and trying to shove them into dark corners of my mind. I'm essentially saying to myself: "I want to do whatever possible for you to only be happy." That's a lot of pressure and can birth shame when sadness inevitably arises.

We must allow ourselves to enjoy the 7, breathing into it with the same knowingness and acceptance and surrender we work so hard to have when in a 1-5 space.

This too will pass. The sooner we accept that fact rather than try to prevent it, the sooner we settle into a nice flow with life. The ups and downs and boring in-betweens become easier to ride. The state of acceptance rather than aversion makes the waves less choppy, the hallway periods seem easier, and we can even start experiencing a sprinkle of 7+ while we are in a rough patch[51]. Why? Because we recognize that we are where we are, *and we learn to be okay with that.* Allowing and relaxing into the present moment rather than trying to wrestle it brings me immense peace.

It's all impermanent.

Remembering impermanence while I'm quasi-enjoying life used to induce panic. Now, I remind myself: I've been to a 7 before, and I'll be here again. I've survived 100% of my shittiest days, and I'm actively working to make my **1-4's** easier to navigate. I've got this.

Honestly, it's a good thing that this high won't last. If it did, we'd likely adapt to it and it would become boring, leaving us seeking a higher high. No matter how hard we try to cling onto a joyful moment, it won't last.

And that's okay.

The natural ebb and flow of human existence is what allows us to appreciate the other parts of it. Additionally, the more we try to keep ourselves feeling a certain way or prevent ourselves from feeling another way, the more susceptible we become to spiraling downward. I think it's because we're trying to direct the show rather than letting

---

[51] That's a lot of metaphors in a single sentence. Apparently, we're riding waves through a hallway that exists in a pumpkin patch.

ourselves be part of it. And that's a job none of us mere flesh sacks were designed for.

It's not your job to control life and everyone in it. All you can control are your actions and, when possible, your attitudes. Each moment is impermanent, even life itself. While this might feel doomy and gloomy, truly understanding impermanence yields the most delicious sense of freedom.

Make a list of stuff you enjoy.

A 7 is about the time when I reconnect with hobbies and people I like, and it becomes easier to feel things like gratitude and fun. If this is the case for you, awesome. *Use this to your advantage.*

Make a list of what you know gives you the warm fuzzies, of adventures you'd like to take, or of things you know help you feel held and seen when you're on the Struggle Bus.

Also, think back to how you've felt during a Valley or Brain Storm, and ponder what you would realistically have the wherewithal to do if you hit a Valley again. When feeling a 7, it could sound great to hike a mountain or go kayaking or travel. When in a **1-4** mindset, though, it may be more feasible to do things like go on a walk around the neighborhood, drink a cup of tea, take a bubble bath, or watch a favorite movie.

You know yourself better than anyone. You know what you enjoy (and don't enjoy), and you know what your motivation level is when in challenging mindsets. (And if you don't "know" this yet, you're learning!)

One of the recommended tasks for a **2** headspace is to do stuff you know you enjoy even though it may not feel enjoyable when struggling (page 89). Similarly, there's a subsection for a **5** headspace called "There's this alleged thing called fun" (page 178) with a similar vibe.

So, make this list for Future You. Add it to those sections (or other sections, if those are more resonant), or save it on your phone.

Look at you, being kind to Future You!

Make a self-care package.

I've shared that impermanence applies to ups just as it does to downs. So, what else can we do to pay it forward to our Future Selves who may be on the Struggle Bus? Do we tend to need extra comfort, extra motivation, or both? Do we benefit from slowing down and relaxing, or perhaps remembering to do basic things like eat food?

I'm all about hoping for the best and preparing for the worst. So, I make sure I have my care package items ready for a potential **1-4** headspace.

JEN'S MENTAL HEALTH
CARE PACKAGE ITEMS:

-TEA
-dark chocolate
-PJ pants (loose)
-ROMANtic comedies
-ESSENTIal oils
-cozy socks
-Highlights magazines

What are yours? Maybe get the tea you like. Buy some crossword puzzles. Have dark chocolate nearby, or a few healthy microwavable meals in the freezer. Maybe this book and your added notes become part of your self-care package. Think of the support you want from others and see how you can give it to yourself.

Maybe you can write yourself a letter for the future based on what you've learned about yourself through viewing the past. Or text yourself a motivational video.

Add this care package information to this book's notebook pages and communicate it with your loved ones. The +1 "Teamwork the care package" subsection (page 231) encourages your Supporter to help with your care package. You can work together to make one for them, too! *We all could use a little extra TLC on rough days.*

You may have to repeat this information (for yourself and your loved ones) multiple times for it to stick. And it may take time to fine-tune your care package. That's okay! Paying it forward in this way is helpful to everyone involved.

Set up future commitments.

I have mixed feelings about this one at this present moment because Past Jen scheduled some stuff for Future Jen (who is now Present Jen) to do. When it came time to do the things, I was pissy and annoyed and all I wanted to do was stay in my jammies and watch romantic comedies while eating homemade gluten-free chocolate chip cookies. But... I went. I followed through on the commitments, even though I was in a **4ish** place, because I trusted my past **7+** self for what she thought would be best for me.

I'm grateful I went out. I mean, I'm most excited that I'm now back home, in my pajamas, with a belly full of cookies, about to watch movies. But I also feel accomplished for having interacted with other humanoids and followed through on my plans.

So, what are a couple fun, upcoming events? Don't bombard yourself or anything. Take it easy while also challenging yourself a bit. Pick something you'll be likely to follow through on no matter your state of mind. Accountability is helpful for me, personally. I like to make plans with someone who's a hardcore extrovert and will light my ass up if I try to cancel. Or I'll sign up for a recurring class of some kind.

My fellow Sensitive friend Brittany told me: "I hate nothing more than the me who makes plans for the future. But even when I'm mad about it, if I can actually make myself do it, I'm usually glad. It's often a class to learn a fun skill. Or dinner or an art exhibit with friends who will understand if I just CAN. NOT."

Honest moment: I do still cancel plans, especially if it's something like a yoga class and there's no specific person holding me accountable. I love a good last-minute cancellation. One of my love languages, personally, is when people cancel plans.

Years ago, I noticed I'd become a habitual plan-canceler. It wasn't cute anymore. People stopped inviting me places, which was a bummer because I liked *being invited* but I didn't want to, y'know, actually go and interact with humans.

I loved the *idea* of attending a future, non-existent event. But on the days leading up to the event, I'd sink deep into depression and panic, hoping for a stomach virus, a flat tire, or another global pandemic so I wouldn't have to attend.

Normally, canceling gave me immediate relief, followed by a wave of guilt and embarrassment and retroactive FOMO (fear of missing out).

I wanted to *want to* show up more consistently. I simply felt like I couldn't, like Past Jen and Future Jen were always fighting each other. So, I started keeping track of how I felt after canceling versus how I felt if I kept my commitments.

It irks me to say it, but the data clearly shows that I feel better about myself when I follow through on a plan.

So, what flavor of socialization sounds fun? Consider how your emotional state has historically been over these last handful of months.

Based on this information from Past You: What sort of "fun commitment" feels attainable, even if you're feeling less social when it's time to follow through?

Join a support group.

A support group may seem like a silly recommendation when in a comfortable, content state of a 7. However, I find it easier to interact with people and start to build relationships when I'm feeling **6+**. There are all kinds of support groups. They've got some for alcoholics, addicts, family and children of alcoholics and addicts, people with eating issues or body image issues, survivors of trauma, folks dealing with grief, and so on.

It's helpful to be around people who "get it." While they may not be your tribe or your forever people, you can begin to build a structure of human interaction that will help prevent you from sliding into isolative glory in the future.

I personally found my support group for many years at a martial arts gym. Everyone there felt like family. They cared about me and called me if they hadn't seen me in a couple weeks. If I cried profusely during a class, they loved on me and encouraged me to beat the shit out of the punching bag.

I'm learning (albeit begrudgingly) that **humans need community**. In this super weird, disconnected world, we may have to go out and find it for ourselves.

It could be a gardening club, an improv troupe, a 12-step program, or a weekly virtual meetup to write with a writer friend. Find what works for you.

Replenish reserves.

I admittedly find myself laying off the healthier choices once I feel more comfortable, because I don't have the same fire under my ass to do self-caring things as I did when in a **1-4** place.

I go from: "I'll do whatever it takes to feel okay!" to, "I feel okay so now I will do nothing KTHX."

Pretty please don't give up on self-care. Now is the time to increase it so you can have more than you need. Replenish your reserves.

Think of every bit of self-care as a deposit into your savings account. Future You who finds themselves on the Struggle Bus may need to withdraw some of those reserves to survive the trip.

I have my non-negotiable maintenance items each day that I do no matter how crappy or how fantabulous I feel: pray, make bed, walk dog, shower[52], and I try to do some form of body movement each day. Nothing fancy: three pushups and three minutes of stretching. I may even hula hoop for three minutes if I'm feeling saucy.

It's okay to give yourself a little wiggle room since you're not currently in a crisis, but I challenge you to keep making deposits into your self-care bank account.

---

[52] The fact that I shower every day is a miracle. I used to barely be able to shower once a week. I highly recommend an app called Finch. It gamifies self-care and has helped me a lot with "basic" life things.

Continue humanoid interactions.

Consistency with reaching out to other Earth humans makes it easier to do so during emotional Valleys. Also, it's pretty gosh darn rude to only reach out to friends and family when we're sad or hungry or needy. *Or* to only reach out to them when we're 7+, as if we're not worthy of being witnessed when we're a bit messier. Or as if they just *couldn't handle us* when we're struggling.

I personally find it refreshing to talk with someone who shows up exactly as they are, no matter how messy. It helps me feel less alone in my mess. Some people say they want positive vibes only.

I want authentic vibes only.

So, who haven't you talked to in a while? Is there someone who reached out who you aptly avoided during a Brain Storm, and now you're like: "Ugh it's been too long to respond I'm just going to avoid it forever until they forget I exist."? Reach back out to them!

> Greetings. Apologies for my silence. I was harnessing my inner hermit and hiding from life. How are you?!

It's a great feeling to call someone and say: "How are *you* today?" And then to listen. Not just listen and wait for our turn to talk, but *really hear them.* We're all going through shit, and we all want to feel heard and held.

+1: Teamwork the care package.

*Your loved one's current state: 7 (**The sun is shining**)*

Ahoy, Supporter! The sun is shining a bit more for your loved one. Glorious.

When it comes to supporting a Sensitive person who struggles with low lows, the most common complaint I've heard from a Supporter is: **"I just have no clue how to help them."** Well, jinkies! It's time to work together to prepare for the future, just in case.

Let's talk about a self-care package. This package may have physical items, like crossword puzzles or a favorite treat, but can also have a list to help you know how to best help your Sensitive loved one.

My fellow Sensitives already have a recommendation to put together a self-care package (page 223), and I encourage them to share it with you!

So, let's talk about a little list that you can keep handy (in this book or elsewhere). Maybe we can even call it the "*Ya Basic* Needs" list. (More about this on page 299.)

Ask your Sensitive loved one what their basic needs are during a **1-4** mindset. Here are some of mine, if it helps: *I need to be fed healthy food, I need help interacting with* *humans, and I need someone to boss me around and tell me how to be an adult for a few days.*

Oh also, *I need to be reminded that I'm still lovable even when I'm an unshowered, depressed mess.*

The goal for *Volume Control* is to help these conversations be a teamwork dialogue where *you're both working toward a common goal.* That collaborative space is where the real healing happens.

Dare I say: I think you *both* deserve your own self-care package of goodies. You're allowed to have rough days where you need extra cozy love, too! Go on a date to the grocery store. Combine efforts to make epic care packages.

Here's a spot to add Supporter notes:

Supporter notes

8-10

IN THE GROOVE

(in-the-flow; hopeful; excited)

"All the pain was totally worth it!"

"I wish I could tell future JEN who's struggling: JEN. INSPIRATION WILL BE BACK. Stop trying to force EVERYTHING! Just RELAX and watch some shows and let your brain RESTART and REGROUP. THERE'S always a delicious lesson and REALIZATION that comes from hard times. I SEE that NOW, and I wish I'd trust that MORE during 1-5's."

— JEN at a 9

*Dear Jen at an **8, 9,** or **10**:*

*You're right; inspiration does always come back. You **can** tell your Future Self those things by adding what you've learned to the appropriate sections of this book!*

Also, remember: Things that feel easy to you now were not easy when you were struggling. Be nice to Past Jen. This section shares how to utilize this in-the-groove headspace without becoming a Stage 5 Clinger to it.

Pay it forward to Future You.

Oftentimes, when I'm feeling on top of the world, I decrease my self-care maintenance. I'll drop recovery meetings and exercise less. I'll skip out on meditation. It's okay to play hooky[53] every now and then, but not to omit all self-care actions until I inevitably sink into the Quicksand of Despair.

It may take more maintenance for me to stay afloat than it does for others. I'm learning that *that's okay.* Maintenance has progressively gotten easier with time, practice, and repetition. It used to take me two hours every morning to get to a state of feeling *barely okay.* Now my morning routine is roughly 30 minutes. While this is an

---

[53] Sometimes, playing hooky is necessary for someone like me who can become too hypervigilant.

improvement, it's still a lot compared to friends who have zero morning routine and seem to operate just fine. They wake up, chug coffee, and immediately scroll social media. If I did that, I'd be in a puddle of angst and tears by 11AM.

This is a wonderful reminder that we are all different. Comparison is futile.

I'm doing my best to find the balance between obsessing about self-care maintenance to the point of misery, versus coddling myself and nixing all maintenance because I just want cozy naps foreverrrrr.

Balance is a mystical concept I've yet to fully grasp, by the way. It can seem elusive, like a unicorn or the matching pairs to my socks.

Since I shimmy a bit more toward the nixing-all-maintenance approach when at an **8-10**, I've learned that this is a time when I need to recommit myself to self-care. It's helpful to look at my relationship with myself as if it were a relationship with another person. How confusing would it be for someone to *only* show up for us when we're sad and in need, the way we can often do for ourselves?

I've dated people like that before, who were only super loving when I was miserable. They liked to be the hero and caregiver. When I was doing well, they'd slide away or become whiny themselves, further perpetuating a victim/hero seesaw dynamic.

We can have that relationship dynamic within ourselves as well. If we only do self-loving actions in a reactive and corrective manner, and cease them when we start to feel more balanced, then where is the ongoing encouragement during the 7+ times? Share the love equally!

Ready to use this motivation and inspiration for good? Clean, get on top of mail and bills, reach out to friends, or do that one thing you've been avoiding.

Schedule mandatory relaxation time.

You're not an invincible television superhero. You're a smooshy human with a fallible flesh vehicle. Relaxation is imperative. Without it, you'll inevitably burn out and find yourself revisiting a MAXed out **2**, or even a **0**.

There's a reminder to rest and relax in many of the sections of this book. *The need for recharge doesn't dissipate just because we have our inspiration and motivation back.* I, for one, need the regular reminder that life isn't so serious that I must be constantly working toward something.

Attempting to relax during an **8-10** often results in me feeling restless and uncomfortable. Trying to rest when my brain is amped on life is like trying to get my 5-month-old puppy to sit still during *the zoomies.*

I'm learning that **even a tiny break from output and input can go a long way** toward keeping my brain from overheating.

Only recently, I've started to be able to chill out and rest even when I feel energized. It's helpful for me to play video games (*Bubble Bobble* or *Mario 64* are my go-tos!), color in a coloring book[54], or walk around in my backyard and find colors of the rainbow in nature. These are restful without me having to force myself to lay perfectly still. Movement *can* be relaxing and restful.

Some examples could be: playing tug of war with my dog Floyd, dancing to a favorite song, or putting food on a

---

[54] Might I recommend the *Coloring Book-opotamus* by Jen Butler? I've heard good things. Mainly from my mom.

plate and actually sitting down to eat it (rather than inhaling it while standing in front of the fridge). Or I can simply step away from screens, give my eyeballs and brain a break, and breathe some fresh air. Listen to the birds.

Give it a try. Put on a 15-minute timer and step away from screens. Do something that's relaxing for you. (If you don't yet know what is relaxing or recharging, just try something. Anything!) Focus on your breathing and on each of your physical senses. Even a tiny break is better than putting the pedal to the metal until overheating.

When I plug back into my input or output after a mini break, I find that I have more clarity and stamina! Woo!

Beware of running hot.

If I push myself too hard for too long when I'm at an **8-10**, I'll quickly drop to a **4**. If I don't slow down, I'll soon collapse to a **0**. It's admittedly tough to slow down when I feel focused, because I'm finally able to accomplish tasks I couldn't during a past Brain Storm. I feel like I have rocket shoes on my feet! I don't want to slow down – I want to go faster!

I may feel my burnout headache and ignore it because I love the feeling of the high I get from rapidly getting stuff done.

"Stop immediately when you become aware of signs of overheating" is too big of a goal for me right now. I had to right-size that goal to what feels attainable: *Notice the signs earlier, and listen to them earlier.* At the time of writing this book, I'm continually taking baby steps toward that goal.

I admittedly still fall prey to the cycle of overwhelm, even after a decade of exploring my emotional responses and behaviors. I'll come out of an emotional Valley, suddenly feel energized and fabulous, and then be like, OMIGOD LET US DO ALL THE THINGS. I'll assume that I am always going to have this ample energy and interest in socialization. Or, I'll feel like I must make up for lost time and do as much as I can before the rug again gets pulled out from underneath me. So, I'll reach out to multiple people I avoided during my hermit mode, make *many* plans, sign up for overlapping classes, and so on.

It's great to make plans and to interact with other humans! I recommend those as to-do items throughout *Volume Control*. I'm talking about the mystical concept of balance here. Overcommitting inevitably leads to overwhelm later down the road.

How do we continue to connect with people and make plans *without overcommitting?* Honestly, we learn by doing. We make the plans, and we see how we feel once they come along. We take note of if the plans were too much, not enough, or the *Goldilocks* zone of just right.

I share in section 4 about learning your signs of overheating (page 142). For example: I get a burnout headache in my temples or behind my eyes along with super dry eyes. I talk *reallyreallyreallyfast* and with the intensity and volume of a stage actor projecting their voice to someone in the very back row.

When I start to forget words or struggle to complete thoughts, that's another reminder that my engine (my brain) is running hot.

What are some signs that you're running too hot? Are you willing to listen to the signs and take a break?

Avoid extreme decisions.

During an **8-10**, I have been known to go "I AM AMAZING AND FULLY SUPPORTED BY LIFE!!!" and dive into some commitment without research or thought. Like that time I started a non-profit organization with zero business plan.

I can feel invincible. This is especially prevalent for me in an **11** headspace, though I can also experience it in the **8-10's**. If someone asked me to do a trust fall at a **2** or **3**, I'd promptly exit stage left. If someone asked me to do a trust fall during **8+**, I'd gleefully fall backward without even checking to see if they were ready to catch me.

Listen, I fully support leaps of faith. I've taken quite a few of them. I'm also learning to recognize when I'm flying a bit high and need to sit on giant decisions until the flailing sense of maniacal urgency calms down (normally 48 hours).

If you are suddenly, randomly excited about a big decision or change, consider writing it down to revisit in a couple days. Or, even better, ask a Supporter if they're willing to be a sounding board.

Anxiety lives next door to excitement.

I once read that many people who are feeling relief after a depressive episode are the ones who are more likely to kill themselves. Why? My guess is that it's because they now have a comparison between feeling decent versus feeling lousy, whereas *before* they may have grown accustomed to the discomfort. When the Suck leaves my brain and I hear the birds singing, I can feel completely overwhelmed by the unfairness that I don't get to experience life that way every day. *The joy somehow resparks the Suck.*

When that happens, I used to assume that the up times were some sort of cruel trick played by the universe. Getting freedom from the Suck only to be dunked back under makes it seem like I'm mentally and emotionally drowning. Like I just can't get a full breath.

I don't think life is designed as some cruel trick to be played on only the highly sensitive. There's just too much magic in the world for that to be the case.

If this current dose of feeling *generally good* sparks anxiety in you? Know you're not alone. It's okay. The physical sensations of anxiety are awfully close to the physical feelings of excitement. I joke that they're next-door neighbors or roommates.

Breathe into the physical feelings of the anxiety and see if they shift into more of an excitement. Either way, it's alright. This is all a part of your experience. Witness it, say hi to it, and be willing to learn from it.

This is not a reward or linear.

I've been caught in the trap before of thinking that my happier moments are a result of all my kindness in the past, as if my glimpse of joy today is directly related to all those times I held doors open for old people and let cars merge in front of me when driving.

This is a dangerous mindset for me to be in, thinking that I am being directly rewarded for some good I did. I'll try to recreate the happiness by continuing to do the things my linear mind says resulted in the happiness.

Rather than enjoying the moment for what it is, I'll grab hold of the controls and try to figure out exactly *how and why* this joyful time has arisen. That way, I can recreate it!

Yeah, life is not that linear. I mean, sure. Taking care of ourselves will likely have a direct impact on how we feel in the future. However, I don't think there's some ongoing tally mark system where we're getting graded on every step, every thought, and every feeling... and then either rewarded or punished later.

Ups and downs happen. Sometimes, there's an apparent reason "why." Other times, there isn't. That's okay. Let it go and enjoy this very exact moment, right now. And if enjoyment is still too abstract a concept[55], then at least focus on your breath, wiggle your toesies, and pull yourself into your body, into the present moment.

We're working to stop applying meaning to our uncomfortable feelings, right? Let's try to remove storylines from our comfortable emotions, too. Rather than, "I feel happy in my brain. It must be because I ate broccoli yesterday. I should have nothing but broccoli for the rest of my life!" I challenge you to instead say: "I feel happy in my brain." *The end.*

We don't need the extra meaning. We don't need the storylines. We can simply be with what is happening right now. That is "presence." At least, I think that's presence.

---

[55] Yes, it's possible to be at an **8-10** and not fully enjoy it. We humanoids are emotionally complex!

But now I'm thinking too hard about the meaning of presence and am no longer present.

But I caught it in the moment! Hooray!

Learn.

Perhaps during a low point, you wrote your Future Self a letter of concerns. Maybe during a **3** headspace you wrote an "I'm pissed because…" note (page 114). Now is the time to research, learn more, and prepare so you can handle future situations in a healthier way. Knowing how we feel and react when we're in a Valley is wonderful knowledge to have. Having this information to reference when in the higher numbers allows us to adjust our approach moving forward.

I think it's beautiful to view ourselves as research subjects, in the most compassionate way possible. By shifting my mindset to see life as an experience, a research project, or even an experiment, I am way less hard on myself! It helps me maintain willingness, curiosity, and even a bit of playfulness.

Rather than being stuck in the mindset of: "Oh this is just how I am; I'll never change," we can instead look at past data and use it to better prepare so that we *can* make different choices in the future. We truly can rewrite and retrain even the stickiest of behaviors.

You are a beautiful, messy, unique human. I encourage you to use this **8-10** as an opportunity to learn about yourself, what makes you tick, what lights you up, and whatever else comes to mind and heart.

Support others. Give back.

During a particularly challenging emotional Valley a few years ago, I was sitting with my back against a tree. *It was a miracle that I'd gotten out of my apartment.* I sat there breathing and meditating and, in my meditative state, I heard: "The amount of pain you feel is proportional to the amount of joy you can feel, and how much you can help other people."

I truly believe that I incarnated with the predisposition toward depression and suicidal ideations so that I could learn from the pain, listen to it, learn to embrace life, and ultimately help other people. As my therapist says: "Jen, let's make something beautiful with this pain."

Maybe this book is that beautiful thing?

It's like in recovery meetings I go to: I've learned that no one can help an alcoholic quite like another alcoholic. No one can help a Sensitive quite like another person who knows what it's like to have the volume turned up on life.

This is a hard time for all humans to be alive. And, as hypersensitive creatures, we are constantly inundated with input at a rate we have not yet evolved to handle. There is a lot of pain, a lot of confusion, and a lot of pressure. And even if you feel like you're not far enough along on your journey, you're further on your journey than someone else.

There is someone out there right this very moment who is caught in a painful situation that you have successfully survived in your life. Even if you feel like you're not *healed enough* (whatever that means) to help, you at least can offer an empathetic ear for those who are still struggling.

I believe that the Sensitives — the ones who feel life so deeply — are here to make change. We must support one another, guide one another, and help to adjust our own volume controls so that we can *experience* human existence rather than hide from it.

+1: Nothing is "fixed."

*Your loved one's current state: **8-10 (In the groove)***

Greetings, precious Supporter human! I imagine it's a joy and relief to see your Sensitive loved one back in the swing of things again, engaging with life.

Here's a gentle reminder that *this emotional state is just as much a part of them as the more challenging emotions.* Each emotion rises and falls like the tides.

So, how can you continue to help your loved one during **8-10**? I admittedly had to ask my partner how he helps support these vibes because naturally, I'm like: "I don't need any help from anyone because I'm kind of super awesome, and I totally have a handle on this life thing."

Then, my partner came into my office, took one look at me, and was like: "When was the last time you took a break and got fresh air?" I responded with utmost maturity by stomping with my white tassel cowgirl boots, because I wanted to keep writing this book! *I'm on a roll, dangit! How dare you interrupt my flow state!* He responded with: "I can *see* the gears turning in your head. I feel the pressure emanating from your body. You gotta stop and smell the roses."

And then we went outside, and he literally pointed out flowers and talked about roses. I didn't sniff them, though. I'll be right back.

Okay, I did it. *Look at me, taking my own advice!*

There's nothing for you to necessarily *do* during this state, aside from staying mindful that this is simply another part of the roller coaster of life. There may again be an intense **1-3**. But for now, you can enjoy that your loved one is in the groove.

And, to help prolong the groove, it may be helpful to offer a few reminders to your Sensitive loved one to take a breather. My friend Kait reminds me: "Breathe and hydrate!" I'll take a huge gasp and be like: "Whoa! How long have I been holding my breath?! Holy crap, I'm so thirsty!"

If you find something else that works, I encourage you to add it here:

Supporter Notes

11

KING of THE WORLD

(amped; over-ambitious; seemingly endless energy)

"I'M THE BEST THING SINCE GLUTEN-FREE BREAD."

"I FEEL INSPIRED AF. I CAN DO ANYTHING I SET MY MIND TO!!! LITERALLY ANYTHING!!! I SHOULDN'T SETTLE FOR ANYTHING LESS THAN WHAT I DESERVE!!! I FEEL ENERGIZED AND HAVE NO NEED FOR THIS SILLY BOOK AND ITS SILLY ADVICE BECAUSE I HAVE IT ALL FIGURED OUT!!! SQUEEEEEEE!!!"

- JEN AT AN 11

*DEAR JEN AT AN **11**:*

*HELLO, I AM TALKING TO YOU IN ALL CAPS BECAUSE THAT IS THE LEVEL OF INTENSITY EXPERIENCED AT AN **11**. IT SEEMS LIKE EVERYTHING IS A PARTY AND EXCITED YELLING IS THE ONLY VIABLE OPTION.*

YES, IT FEELS GREAT TO FEEL GREAT. IT FEELS REALLY FREAKING AWESOME.

*IN ORDER TO PREVENT A BIG OL' PENDULUM SWING BACK TO THE **0-3** RANGE, THIS SECTION SHARES HEALTHY WAYS TO KEEP YOUR ATTITUDE IN CHECK.*

Leave it to Batman.

Do you ever imagine being an actual real-life superhero? I do.

I imagine myself helping millions of people and being this profound untouchable human who can learn entire languages in three minutes and kick bad guys' butts. *Think Limitless meets Ironman meets Jesus.*

In my imagination land, I envision myself staying eternally youthful and defying aging due to my positive attitude and general kindness. *Terminally ill people are suddenly cured after I've touched their heads! I'm making*

Ellen DeGeneres laugh while I'm on her show talking about my multiple New York Times bestsellers!

In my *Ellen Show* mental movie, a very tall Jason Segel comes on stage, and I look up and say to him: "You are the Gandalf to my Frodo." And then everyone laughs, and he holds me like a baby.

Yep. It's true. And in that moment, all of the above seems totally attainable. I mean, I get that visualizing the life we want is important. But Jen at an **11** takes it to the next freaking level.

For context: six months into sobriety, while living off credit cards in a tiny apartment, I started a non-profit organization. The tagline was: "One person can change the world." *It was me. I was the one person.*

I rode the high for a few months and then was like: "Oh shit, what have I done? I started a freaking BUSINESS?!" (I ultimately dissolved the business. It was the smart and responsible thing to do.)

If I know that I still struggle to stay on Earth during my **1-3** stages or am still incredibly sensitive and reactive to rejection, maybe I'm not quite ready to commit to something giant like *running an entire non-profit organization that's allegedly going to heal the world.*

Setting goals is important. If one of those goals is to *defy all odds and save the whole world*, that's not realistic, healthy, or sustainable.

We are all here in our little corners of the world with our own individual gifts. We have our own unique interests, passions, and things that inspire us. Stick with *those* things rather than riding your ego all the way into the battlefield with nothing but your three preceding days of joy backing you up.

Take it easy. Do what you can. Leave the rest to Batman.

You're not hot shit.

Hello, you GLORIOUS BEAST of a human! You are so fuh-*reaking* awesome! And yet... it's important to remember that you're not *better* than anyone. I know that I can feel superior when at an **11**. Yeah, that's not a pretty thing to admit, but it's true. I'll think I'm more aware than people or that the universe prefers me over others because I, like, don't litter and they do, or something silly.

I have to remind myself that I'm neither above nor below anyone. So, I'll offer the reminder to you. Imagine I'm singing it to you like an epic impromptu musical, if that makes it more fun.

You are neither above nor below anyone. *Doot de doo!*

You're not above who you were when you were in an emotional Valley a week or month ago. You're not above the friend who seems to be *stuck in negativity.* You're not above the Walmart greeter or the homeless guy or the person stuck in their corporate boxed-in job.

You. Are. Not. Hot. Shit.

Slow it down. Take some deep breaths. A little humility would be super helpful right now. You're a fallible human, and this is merely a wave of feel-good energy.

Others' emotions are still valid.

I've admittedly been guilty of toxic positivity. People have reached out to me when they're struggling and I'm at an **11**, and I'd spew all kinds of positive shit about how much they have to be grateful for and what *I think they should do* from my high and mighty throne of **11-dom**.

This isn't helpful.

Take some deep breaths and ground yourself back on Earth. You do not know everything. You do not know what's best for other people. It's great that you feel great, but be sure that you don't use it as an excuse to act better than people just because you currently "feel better" than they do.

Knock that shit off, fancy pants.

Remember that one time you melted down in the grocery store and gutturally screamed profanities while punching the self-checkout machine because it wouldn't accept your coins, and your then-boyfriend had to tackle you to the floor? And then you kicked the sliding doors off their hinges?

Oh wait, that was me.

EVEN SO. The logic remains. You have had rough times. And, if you've ever talked with one of those obnoxiously optimistic people who are spewing Deepak Chopra fortune cookie insight at you while you just need someone to listen? You know how lousy it feels.

Make a commitment to treat other people with respect, listen to them, and **honor where they are**. You very well may be there again, too.

Slow it down, Broseph.

You'll see regular reminders to unplug and rest throughout *Volume Control*. Maybe you're the Royalty of Rest and awesome at it. I am not. And when we've flung to an **11** space, we can just as easily swing back to a **1-3**.

Or, we may keep pushing ourselves and burning so hot that we promptly fizzle into a **0**, when our whole system burns out. You are not a robot or a machine. You are a soul riding around in a flesh vehicle called a body. This body houses a big, beautiful, squishy brain. Your body, brain, soul, and beyond need rest to stay healthy.

Please release your foot off the gas pedal, just a bit. Take some deep belly breaths. Put your bare feet on the earth. Or plop those precious toesies into some cozy socks or monster slippers.

We need you here. Pushing yourself to the redline zone may very well result in burnout or a breakdown and a bunch of corrective maintenance.

Be proactive and **make time to slow down**.

Note: Slowing down when I'm in an **11** headspace felt very unnatural and uncomfortable at first. Trying to "rest" just pissed me off. I felt like a hyper Border Collie being forced into a cage. But, over time and with a lot of practice, I'm learning how to take *mini recharges* even when I'm at full energy. This helps me sustain my energy for longer and prevents the big dips to **1-3** due to overdoing it.

My battery seems to recharge more quickly when I'm at an **8+**. A five-minute breathing meditation can fully reset my brain and calm my nervous system, whereas I'll need *two days of sleep* to replenish when I'm at a **2**.

Even if you don't want to rest or it feels impossible to do so, maybe you can at least slow down your breathing and movement for a few minutes.

Shake it off.

Have you ever seen dogs shake their bodies after a stressful or exciting situation, or after meeting someone they didn't really like? I've noticed my dogs doing this, and I have started shaking my entire body each time I see them doing it. Even if we're around someone else. I'm like: "They can clearly feel something I can't. I'm shaking it off, too!"

Excess energy feels like an increasing pulsation within my chest and cells, eager to be let out into the world. This can feel uncomfortable, especially when I'm trying so damn hard to be mindful of *not overdoing it*.

I've learned that I'm more apt to burn out when I overexert *mental energy* rather than physical energy. This mental exertion may be via creative output, posting videos online, responding to twenty emails, or starting another screenplay while also writing three others.

When I'm recharged and super energized, it feels like I have way too much energy to be able to mentally exert it all. My sweet brain isn't intended to process that much output so quickly. Thus, I'm learning how good it is for me to be *physically exhausted.*

Not the *existential dread* sort of exhaustion, but the exhaustion and quiet mind that comes from physically exerting a buildup of energy.

If the subsections about rest and relaxation feel impossible or miserable, consider trying a form of physical activity first. A long hike will do it for me, or even 10-15 minutes of intense cardio. If nothing else, I'll turn on a song and awkwardly flail my body to the music, like a dog shaking its body, but for a solid three minutes... to the tune of *Rage Against the Machine.*

It's important to meet our emotions where they are, to meet our energy level where it is.

What to do with all these vibes.

Are you jacked full of energy and amped on life? Awesome. Me too. (Cue **11**-inspired cyber dance party!)

Let's use the energy for good.

In what ways can you help another in need[56] or someone important to you? Can you research a cause you're passionate about and see how to volunteer? Head to

---

[56] Without spewing toxic positivity, trying to rescue or micromanage them, and without overdrafting your bank account.

a recovery meeting and offer to set up beforehand or clean up afterward? Do something super thoughtful for your loving Supporter?

Similarly, in what ways can you help Future You in need? Can you add more to your Brain Storm care package (page 223)? Make a silly video for your Future Self who may be feeling blue? Search your favorite content creators and bookmark some of their videos for a stormier, Future You to watch?

I've also found that, during an **11**, it's much, much easier for me to take any action that seemed terrifying in the **1-4's**. I'm currently doing an Avoidance Journey where I'm tackling 30 tasks I'd been avoiding on my journey to pursuing my dreams (publishing this book is one of the tasks). Most of the avoidance tasks have a similar theme of me reaching out to industry professionals, marketing myself, and generally *putting myself out there*. These tasks are very challenging to do when I'm in a **1-4**. When I shimmy into an **8-10**, though, some of the tasks suddenly seem effortless!

Is there something you currently feel brave enough to do that Past You was too scared or insecure to try?

The same goes for basic self-care tasks. During the Suck, I'll *logically know* that going on a hike with my dog will help me, but it feels impossible. So, now that I'm at an **11**, I may take advantage of that inspired energy, pack

Floyd into the car, buckle his seatbelt, and head to the woods. (This is good physical exertion, too!)

I like to think of our emotions as the fuel, and our body as the vehicle. If you were to use this amped excitement as fuel, where would you want to drive?

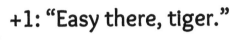

♥ +1: "Easy there, tiger."

Your loved one's current state: **11 (King of the world)**

Howdy, Supporter friend! When I'm at an **11**, I have the energetic presence of a very hyper Border Collie who hasn't been on a walk in weeks. When I try to slow down, it feels like I'm forcing that Border Collie in a cage. I actually get angry. *I just want to run and be free!* But if I run too hard, commit to too much, and skip out on basic things like food and sleep, *I **am** going to crash.*

I don't love admitting this fact. Because in this current mindset, I feel freaking great. I'm getting so much done. I CAN DO ALL THE THINGS.

No, I can't.

My Supporters *always* see impending burnout signs before I do. Oh, and apparently, it's helpful for me to learn to be *receptive* to their reminders to slow down. There are times when my partner is like: "Take a breath. It's not a race." And I do all the deep breathing possible so as not to scream in his face:

After years of him witnessing most of my **11's** toppling into a **0**, I've begrudgingly begun to realize that he may have a clearer grasp on reality when I'm at an **11**. So, here are some examples of what he says to me that I'm learning to be receptive to. Maybe you can try some of these with your Sensitive loved one during their **11**:

- *Slow it down. This isn't a race.*
- *Take a breath. Or three.*
- *Let's make a list of all the things you want to do and see what we can prioritize.*
- *Not everything is gonna get done today, and that's okay.*
- *Let's go outside and get some fresh air.*

(And so on.)

Your volume control loved one may not listen to you the first time (or the tenth time) you remind them to slow down. But eventually, once they learn more about their cycles and tendencies toward running too hot and burning out, they'll hopefully become more willing to listen to your advice to *take it easy there, tiger.*

Other thoughts about this section? Plop them in this little note:

O

BURNOUT

(zapped; exhausted; zombie mode)

"Overdid it. Again. Brain is goop."

"I CAN baRELy stRiNG a
coHERENt SENtENcE togetHER.
WoRds aRE HaRd. I HAVE ZERO
capacity to ENGaGE iN basic
HumaN pLEASANtRiES. NEEd to
tuRN off bRaiN aNd watcH
sHows."

— JEN at a Ø

*Dear Jen at a **0**:*

So, you redlined life until your brain overheated. Hey, it happens. And it's occurring less and less than it used to. Please be gentle and nurturing with yourself. Eat what you need to eat. Sleep as much as you need to sleep. Watch shows or read books that don't at all challenge your brain or nervous system.

Now is a time for rest until your brain restarts. And it will restart; it always does. This section shares different approaches to help you take it easy and recharge.

Activate easy mode.

You know in video games when you can choose the difficulty level? Any sort of self-awareness or self-healing is expert-level shit. *Big boss* vibes. During burnout, I've learned that I need to press pause on the difficult stuff and transition to easy mode.

What does easy mode look like?

For me? *Full-on nurturing and indulgence.* I order DoorDash even though one meal is half the cost of a grocery run[57].

I give the middle finger to the shower. I take the dogs into the backyard rather than for a walk around the neighborhood. If it's doable, I may prepare a fancy bath for myself and give my feetsies a much-deserved massage.

I shared earlier in the book about daily non-negotiables. These are the maintenance items that I do each day no matter how I feel... *unless I'm burnt out.* Burnout is a sign that I've overdone it and need to STOP.

I gather my desired feel-good items from my Brain Storm care package list (page 223), such as loose PJ pants, cozy socks, and dark chocolate. I crawl in bed. I turn on the TV. I watch a show or movie I've already seen, or anything that I know will bring zero emotional or mental challenge to my brain. (Think: cheesy rom-com where you know from the first scene what's going to happen, instead of a suspenseful horror movie with clown-induced, butt-puckering jump scares.)

The time of easy mode is not a forever thing. Frankly, it can't be. Otherwise, I'd merge and become one with the bed, run out of money from all the to-go food ordered, and

---

[57] An early 2000's grocery run. Nowadays, $50 gets me an organic bell pepper and one pack of butt wipes.

I'd lose my job and relationships. But, for a day or three, it's doable hotwise.

Also, as I'm writing this section, I have a voice in my head saying: "Jen, you should nurture yourself and indulge in the delicious self-care you just mentioned, *even when you're not burnt out.*" You're probably right, voice in my brain. But I, too, am a work in progress. So, respectfully, get off my lady nuts.

What responsibilities can you omit today? What sort of nurturing yumminess sounds good? How can you make your day as easy as possible? Do it. The faster you rest your brain, the faster it heals and comes back online.

Exit browser windows.

When a coworker shares their screen in a video call, I like to count how many browser tabs they have open. *And then silently judge them.* Sometimes, they have so many open that only a sliver of each website logo shows up!

I think that's how our brains get, too. We're thinking about and planning and analyzing so many things all the damn time. Not to mention the incessant input from social media and the news and the neighbor's dog who won't stop barking.

Think about when your phone is running slowly and you check how many apps you have open, and it's an outrageous number. That means it's time to close out of the browser tabs and apps. Maybe even restart the little fella.

If a computer or phone is running slowly and you check with tech support, they're gonna ask if you've restarted it. Restarting a device clears the cache, fixes glitches, closes background processes, and so on.

This is what we need to do with our brain and bodies when we overheat.

What can I exit out of? What can I cancel or omit from my daily to-dos without hardcore repercussions? What big projects and plans can Future Jen think about instead of Present Jen?

I close out of the browser tabs in my mind of all my projects, ideas, dreams, and fears. And then I watch baking shows or something that requires very little from my brain. Even if the stories or ideas keep popping up, with practice I'm able to lower their volume into an ignorable background noise. **What can you exit out of?**

Have to vs. want to.

I love to-do lists. I have to-do lists reminding me to complete other to-do lists. I can't tell you how many planners I've purchased and used religiously for three gloriously organized weeks, only to suddenly forget they exist until I buy a new one the next year.

I spent a lot of my life very sick. Not only with debilitating depression, but I also had an autoimmune disorder called BII (Breast Implant Illness). As a result, for many years, I could truly barely get out of bed. I moved home with my parents in my early thirties. I was in so much pain and so exhausted, and I felt like I was watching life pass me by.

After getting those toxic bags of goo ripped out of my chest, detoxing my body and mind, and dedicating myself to all flavors of recovery, something magical happened. *I started to get my energy and mental clarity back.* I began believing that my dreams may actually be attainable after all! I started to feel a kind of panicky motivation.

Maybe it's gratitude, but to me it feels more like desperation and gratitude had a secret love child after a wild night in Vegas. I find myself sprinting to get as much done as I possibly can, because there's part of me that feels like I need to make up for lost time, and another part of me that feels like I'm on borrowed time.

For a while, this sprinting pace feels good, almost like a high from a drug. But it's never enough. If I accomplish ten things today, I'm going to want to accomplish twelve tomorrow, fifteen the next day, and so on. As a result, I inevitably find myself waking up one day to a giant to-do list that feels like an elephant on my chest.

I panic and sink into overwhelm because, in my mind, "There's SO much I *have to* do!"

Here's what I've learned, though. There are very, very few things we actually *have to* do. "Oh, I have to post a video today because I said I would. Also, I need to call my friend back and respond to those emails and cook a proper meal."

Actually, *no*, Jen. None of those are necessities for survival. Post the video another day. Reschedule with the friend. Snooze the emails. Order DoorDash or eat a peanut butter and jelly sando.

There's an exercise in the **Supporter** subsection at the end of the book called "Must-do, may-do" (page 300) that encourages them to help you decipher must-dos (non-negotiable responsibilities) versus may-dos (what you can set aside for now). If you need the assistance of a Supporter and they're available to help, consider tagging them in.

Whether this is a solo or collaborative adventure, here's my task for you. If your sweet, crispy, burnt-out brain is like: "Ugh, I have to do ABC and XYZ..." I challenge you to get rigorously honest with yourself about what actually *needs* to be done to keep you (and living beings you care for, if applicable) alive and well.

It's surprisingly a much shorter list than you'd think.

Hard no!

My fellow fans of the Canadian show *Letterkenny* will likely be familiar with this phrase. As a recovering people-pleaser, the very idea of saying "no" to someone still brings minor heart palpitations. *If I say no, won't they be mad and hate me and their lives will be ruined and then MY life will be ruined?* Turns out, um... no. (And if someone is a jerk because we protect our time and energy by saying "no," then that's their own shit to deal with. Let's refuse to let them piss in our cosmic Cheerios.)

Learning to say no has been especially important as a writer and content creator. For over a decade, I've shared my words with the world. And only in the last couple years did I start gaining a following. Prior to that, I think my only consistent reader was my dad. And his response was normally: "This is great, Jen! I have one question. Will you ever write about anything maybe... *less sad*?"

Probably not, Poops[58]. *throws glitter*

Nowadays, people ask me to read and edit their work, help them through an emotionally tough spot, or hold them accountable. I love that people are hungry for this! And at first, I said yes. *A lot.* But I'm learning that this isn't sustainable for me on a large scale.

It has been a similar learning experience with how I show up for my partner and his kids. I wanted to be everything to them (and everyone else) all of the time. This behavior, naturally, leads to burnout. Once my brain is crispy, I'm no help to anyone.

But here's a cool plot twist.

I've learned to see burnout as a gift, because when my mental battery is at ~3%, *saying no becomes a necessity for survival.* I no longer have the capacity to take care of

---

[58] Autocorrect once changed Pops to Poops and now my dad's nickname is forever Poops.

people's feelings. Heck, I can barely string together full sentences. So, rather than beautifully written paragraphs of why *I am so very sorry that I can't do a thing for someone and here are the 30 reasons why*, my sweet burnout brain is like: "No. I'm not interested."

Gasp! What? Isn't that mean?

No. *It's clear.*

If the people in your life are accustomed to you being a "yes" person, there may be a bit of backlash when you start setting boundaries. (If not from them, your *inner guilt gremlin* may whisper sweet nothings in your brain, bullying you about saying no.) *Tough titties, guilt gremlin!* We're in burnout right now, and our priority is to rest and replenish. We may need to cancel or postpone commitments. It's not the end of the world.

Use this as a time to practice your "hard no." You may even start to notice what energizes you versus drains you. When my body and brain are depleted, it becomes very clear what I do and do not want to do, or what I can and cannot do.

What are you most eager to cancel? What commitment elicits the most existential angst? Is there anything that feels nurturing or like it'll recharge your battery? This is important data to write down.

Future You with a more charged battery can take a look at this insight and do a better job at saying yes to the energizing commitments and "hard no!" to the draining ones.

Welcome to Cozy Town.

Whenever the kiddos and I put on PJs, climb under the weighted blanket, and snuggle stuffies, we deem it *Cozy Town, USA*. It's one of those silly things I said one time six years ago that everyone has adopted as a regular part of their vocabulary.

When I'm burnt out, I know it's time to remove the tight or itchy clothes and replace them with ratty pajama pants, a sweatshirt, and cozy socks. I need to stop caring about looking pretty or attractive, or being anything aside from comfortable. My brain and body clearly need nurturing, and sputtering over to Cozy Town, USA is what my nurturing looks like.

What is the landscape like in your Cozy Town? Do you have a favorite blanket, book, movie, song, or stuffy? **Here is your permission to get as cozy as possible.** Yep, that's right: You're allowed to chill out. Rest doesn't mean you've failed at adulting or that you're wasting your life away. There is no guilt, shame, or "less than" to be found anywhere in Cozy Town. Trust me; I checked. So, set those aside for this restful part of your adventure.

And hey, if life's responsibilities won't let you lay around and watch shows all day, that's okay. You can at least find the most comfortable clothes and shoes, or wear or carry something that feels nurturing and loving to you.

No matter what, I'm confident you can make your day at least 5% cozier.

Ease back into it.

If I activate easy mode, exit mental browser windows, say hard no, and hang out in Cozy Town, my mental battery will start recharging. Historically, as soon as I felt at a solid 30%, I'd be like, "Welp! Time to get back to sprinting!" And then inevitably find myself burnt out again in a few hours.

HARUMPH.

Think of when a cell phone battery dies and it's, like, properly drained. *This is burnout.*

Then, you plug it in, and that little battery icon pops up which means, "Hi, human person. I'm charging but don't effing touch me right now because I literally can't EVEN." After leaving the phone plugged in, the percentage of charge will steadily increase. But, if we unplug it and open 17 games and apps and text messages, the charge won't last long.

This is what can happen if we sprint back into life once we start to feel ourselves recharge after burnout. *So, this is why we must ease back into life.*

When you start to feel more like yourself, please keep resting and recharging. Continue doing what you can to nurture and coze and love on yourself. We're cracking open the door rather than flinging it wide open. We're walking and trotting the horse to warm them up before we ask them to gallop in a race. We're letting the cell phone stay plugged in as long as possible so we can get back to very important things like watching cat videos.

+1: Mashed potatoes and a show.

Your loved one's current state: 0 (Burnout)

So, Supporter... it appears as though your Sensitive loved one overdid it again and is burnt out. Oopsy daisy!

My mom used to say to me: "Stop reading all those how-to books. You need something simple. Read fiction. Watch a silly show. Your brain is clearly tired and needs to rest. Watch or read something fun and easy."

Even my therapist and sponsor recommended things like smut and easy, dumb TV. I thought they were unspiritual, unaware people. But one day about seven years ago, when I was so burnt out that I genuinely couldn't formulate sentences, my big brother showed up to my house. He brought food that he'd cooked, a beautiful blue orchid, and a DVD player that also connected to Netflix. He set it all up and turned on *Good Burger*, a delightfully ridiculous movie that we watched together as kids.

I sat there and ate mashed potatoes while watching *Good Burger*. By the end of the movie, I was able to formulate a sentence.

Sometimes, the brain just needs the basics: rest and nutrition. And *we may need help knowing what that looks like*.

So, what are some really precious, easy, indulgent, feel-good things that can help recharge your burnt out loved one's battery?

Here's a lil' piece of paper to add any Supporter ideas:

SUPPORTER NOTES

THE SUPPORTER

"I want to be helpful, but I don't know how. Do you want me next to you, or do you want me to go away? Did I cause this in some way? Will it always be like this? How can you be depressed when your life is so good? Just help me understand, so I know what to do."

- Supporter

*Dear **Supporters**:*

May all flavors of your preferred divinity bless you, you sweet and caring soul. Supporting a Sensitive who struggles with volume control is a heavy lift. It's not for the faint of heart. But, we love who we love. And, I may be partial, but I believe that the folks with the volume turned up on life have the capacity to be wildly caring, aware, creative, vibrant people.

Good news: There are ways to make the challenging times more bearable for you and for your loved one.

I wrote this section with the help of my partner, my mom, and some of my dearest friends whose loved ones struggle with volume control issues. Note that this isn't a perfect science, and the following tips and tricks are based on my own experience and that of the folks I interviewed.

Think of this entire process like learning to dance or even learning a new language. It's tough enough to do solo. When you add a partner into the mix, there are all sorts of kinks to work out. But it can be done!

As always, take what you like and leave the rest.

A quick note for lovely Supporters: I prefer conversational analogies and playful phrases over medical language. So, rather than calling something a depressive episode, I normally say: the Suck; the Ouch; the Struggle Bus; the Quicksand; the Valley; the Brain Storm... and so on. These phrases are more colorful and fun for me. Just a heads up to prep you for your reading!

To help *you*

Put on your oxygen mask first.

First and foremost, let's talk about the importance of taking care of your health. Yes, *your* health, epic Supporter person.

Believe it or not, not everything is about the struggling loved one.

You still exist, and your brain and body need and deserve nourishment and care.

I know that when I'm in a heavily depressive Valley, I can turn into a bit of a black hole, as if I'm the center of a universe where everyone else orbits me. If I'm not receptive to help or am stuck in the sticky shit of victimhood, any energy someone gives me simply disappears into the black hole.

If someone keeps giving and giving, an otherwise healthy person can quickly become depleted or desperate.

How do you know if you're being depleted by your efforts? Here's what my partner says:

> - Make sure your own basic self-care needs are squared away before trying to help your loved one. You can't give from an empty cup.
>
> - If you start to feel your loved one's negativity as your own, that's a sign that you need a breather.

Focus on how you feel. Some days, you'll have more to give. Others, you may be wiped out and not able to show up in the way your loved one wants. *That's okay.*

You can't love us into a state of health. If you take care of us to the point where it's a detriment to you, it's also a detriment to us.

This may mean setting boundaries and being more direct than you're accustomed to being. An example of a boundary may be: "I can tell you're struggling, and I wish I could help, but I'm wiped out and need to focus on keeping myself healthy today." You taking care of yourself sets a good example for your loved one, and holds them accountable to learning how to maintain their own self-care.

There are amazing 12-step programs that help teach folks healthy boundaries. I also recommend some great books in the **Resources** section.

You can't fix this.

There isn't any magical solution. For the sake of everyone involved, pretty please don't act like you have one. I've heard all sorts of recommendations. I've tried each of them and I promise you: it's just not that simple. We can make daily adjustments and heal bit by bit. We can rewrite storylines in our head and learn to regulate our nervous system. But, we're not an equation to solve. We're beautifully complex humans trying our best to get through each day.

It's not your job to fix this, to fix us. **There's nothing to fix.** This is how we experience life, and it may be different from how you experience life. We're willing to learn new ways to cope and regulate, but it isn't an overnight thing. So, please be patient with us. Also, be patient with yourself. It's normal to want to fix stuff, but in this case, it's a futile effort.

Acceptance will be far more helpful than trying to figure us out, fix us, or throw a magical supplement at us.

Here's what I mean by acceptance. I used to think that "acceptance" of a situation meant I was adopting the situation as my forever reality. *Welp, I guess this is my life now!* But accepting a challenging situation is not the same as admitting defeat and giving up.

The challenge is to accept the fact that your loved one is currently struggling, and *you cannot fix it.*

Right now, that is what's happening. It's not about giving up or conceding that life will forever be this way. I encourage you to simply acknowledge where things stand right now. This gives you a starting point.

There are ways you can help or encourage them (some of which I share in this book and others you'll learn through experience). But it is not your job to change their emotions or exhaust yourself by saving them from their Struggle Bus times.

Take a deep breath and loosen your mental grip on the situation. Yes, your loved one may be in the Suck right now. **The Suck shall pass.** And, when it does, you can work together to come up with a game plan of how to handle life a little bit differently next go-around.

You're allowed to be happy.

Misery loves company, and I know that when I'm in a Valley of depression, I can feel like other people's happiness is *rude* or an attack on me.

Just because your loved one is struggling doesn't mean you have to.

Your emotions don't have to mirror one another. It's okay for you to be happy while they struggle. You enjoying life doesn't mean you're not supporting them. It means you're taking care of yourself and continuing to live your own life.

You are allowed to be happy.

It's not your fault.

If your Sensitive loved one is in the Suck, please try super-duper hard not to take it personally. This task can feel impossible and definitely takes practice. But – trust me – you have zero control over this person's volume control issues. My mom says that this is especially challenging for her as a parent, because she literally *made* me! I'm like: "Even so, Mom, I'm my own individual person. How I experience life isn't anyone's fault. Not even yours!"

Even if your loved one blames you or projects onto you in their reactive time of the Suck, their Brain Storm has nothing to do with you. Do what you can to lovingly detach.

When I say "lovingly detach," I don't mean that you should abandon ship. Detaching doesn't mean that you don't care. Rather, loving detachment is a way of loving someone while encouraging their autonomy and your own.

It can be helpful to think of the situation like someone experiencing a tummy virus or a kid having a temper tantrum. Rather than cancel all plans to try and cure the tummy virus, you'd likely offer some extra TLC and then let the virus run its course. And sometimes, when a kid is in a temper tantrum, we have to wait it out without reacting too strongly.

Also, even if you have a rough day and don't respond to a situation as well as you'd like? *You're human!* You're allowed to make mistakes or say the "wrong" things. We can handle it. I mean, we may have a temper tantrum or cry in an empty bathtub, but we'll be fine. We're survivors.

What I mean by this is: Even if, from the outside, a Sensitive loved one's meltdown looks like it's your fault? *It's rarely that simple.* Listen: **Disagreements happen**. Tension occurs in relationships. That's all natural and, in the right context, *healthy*. Our reactions may simply be bigger than yours. Or it may take us longer to recover from an argument.

But by the same token, don't be a cruel jackass and then, when your loved one gets rightfully upset, be like: "JEN BUTLER SAID IT WASN'T MY FAULT." That's a copout. *And I really hope the folks taking the time to read this section don't favor that type of behavior.*

I genuinely hope you find a yummy balance of being kind and loving to one another, while also staying in your own "lane" so as not to drag each other down.

If your volume control loved one is having a tantrum or meltdown, please be gentle and patient *with yourself.* **You** may need a little extra nurturing.

There's nothing you can say.

When I was at my worst and wanted to leave this earthly realm, there was nothing anyone could have said to convince me to stay. Similarly, now that I've decided to stay, there's nothing anyone can say to convince me to leave. Just because we hypersensitive humans may struggle with the day-to-day doesn't mean we're weak or soft. In fact, we're incredibly strong. We just need to learn how to use that strength *for* rather than *against* us.

I had to fall to my lowest of lows before I made the commitment to stay. **No one person had the power to save me.**

The reason I say this is because most loved ones walked on eggshells around me for decades. They were afraid if they said the "wrong thing" that I'd spiral into the Quicksand of Despair and kill myself, and it'd be all their fault. I hate to say it but, no one has that much power over me. Plus, my battle was with myself, not with others.

Even when internet trolls say the cruelest things ever, I'm like: "Ha! I used to say and think WAY worse things about myself. Be more creative, chucklenuts!"

Obviously, don't purposely be a jerk to someone who's struggling. Use your common sense. This section is more so for the folks who may feel like they're constantly tiptoeing around their Sensitive loved one, afraid that any wrong word or wrong step is going to be the end of the end.

We highly sensitive people with MAXed out volume knobs are incredibly tenacious. Since we've remained on Earth thus far (and have survived 100% of our days here), there's clearly a spark within us that will fight to stay alive.

Please give us the space and freedom to live our lives and make our own decisions. Obviously, if there's a genuine mental health crisis and you need to step in or seek outside help, do so[59].

But not every uncomfortable situation or meltdown is a true crisis. You and your loved one must work together to discover what is and isn't a crisis.

Take it easy on yourself. You're only human.

You don't have to receive that.

When I'm in the Ouch, I see life through a lens of negativity. That is my camera view of reality. If I share my skewed point of view with my Supporter and they're like: "Actually, life is pretty awesome." I may get pissy at them. I may be snarky. I don't love this behavior, but I've witnessed myself do it before.

My partner has gotten really, really good at dodging my shitty attitudes. I used to get annoyed that I was no longer eliciting the emotional response from him that I desired. Like a kid misbehaving to get attention, when I stopped getting the reaction I wanted, I eventually stopped being as pissy and snarky to him.

If your loved one is trying to hand you a gift box of doo doo attitude, you don't have to receive it.

---

[59] Text or call 988 (U.S. only), or visit https://988lifeline.org/chat/

What does this look like in practice?

When my friend reaches her limit with her highly sensitive husband's negativity, she'll say: "I'm full. My negativity tank is full. I can't take anymore right now. Come back later."

Maybe you implement a "pause button" where you table a topic and come back to it later.

Or perhaps it's an internal skillset to work on within yourself, where you learn how to listen to your loved one's complaints without taking them on as your own. (Practice, practice, practice.)

Boundaries are imperative. It may feel scary to set a boundary with a hypersensitive or reactive person. There may even be a temper tantrum backlash afterward. But boundary-setting is a gift to *everyone* involved. It's a muscle to build. I've found 12-step programs and therapy to be super helpful for learning to set boundaries, as well as respecting boundaries of others.

To help *you* help *them*

Help with the basics.

Honestly, when life is extra loud and I'm riding the Struggle Bus, the basic day-to-day necessities may feel impossible. Food, water, hygiene. Those things are simply nowhere near the front of my mind.

You know how when you have the flu, your energy is totally zapped and your standards for hygiene suddenly plummet? *Yeah, it's a lot like that.*

For me, the hardest basic need to handle is food. The thought of creating a meal for myself can feel so daunting, it brings me to tears. My closest friends know that, when I'm in the Ouch, food helps. My partner will make something yummy for me, or has even helped walk me to the shower and put on fresh clothes if my brain is crispy. My friend's partner brushes her hair for her when she's in the Suck, *which is so sweet it makes my eyeballs sweat.*

Each person is different, but I think food and water are pretty universally appreciated when in the Suck.

It's worth a conversation with your loved one, even if they're not currently struggling, so you can discover what they most need help with during a Brain Storm.

The +1 subsection "Teamwork the care package" (page 231) also talks more about curating a "*Ya Basic* Needs" list.

Must-do, may-do.

You might have kiddos or, like, an entire life going on outside of the volume control loved one's current Brain Storm. Life doesn't stop just because we Sensitives are having a rough day with our volume knob MAXed out.

My partner gives me a lot of grace and helps carry the weight of responsibilities around the house when I'm struggling. But something that's been surprisingly helpful for me is when he holds me accountable. He and I discuss the *must-dos* (non-negotiable responsibilities) and the *may-dos* (stuff that can be put off without hardcore repercussions).

There's something about someone expecting me to be a responsible adult that draws me into that world, no matter how impossible it may feel. An example is that my partner has two kids. I swore I would never have kids because I didn't think I could handle it because of how sensitive I was. Plot twist: I fell in love with a man with two kids. And they light up my life. Life is funny like that.

We were really concerned about how my depressive episodes and Struggle Bus times would impact his children. We almost ended our relationship over it. I mean, he already has two kids. *He doesn't need me as his third one.*

We've thankfully found a balance with how honest we are with the kids, what we share with them, and what the expectations are for everyone involved. (One of the kiddos is super physically affectionate and I've learned it's okay for me to say: "I'm touched out. It's not your fault. It's just my body today. Can we sit next to each other but not on top of each other?" And she's like, "Oh! Okay!" This honest communication has been a game-changer.)

My partner helps me decipher which tasks or responsibilities I can cancel (the "may-dos").

But if it's a kid's birthday or it's snuggle time before bed or a kiddo is having a rough day? That is a must-do, and the expectation is that I step outside of myself and show up for them. My insides may be screaming, and life may be super loud. I may feel sensory overload and touched out, *but I can still show up*, just as I am. Messy, unshowered, unfunny.

In fact, some of the best conversations have happened with the kids and with my partner when I'm in the Suck, because I don't have the capacity to filter every little thing I say.

So, perhaps you can have this *must-do/may-do* conversation with your loved one.

And then, the fun part: *Hold them accountable, even when they're struggling.* As someone who used to hide from all responsibilities and people, I can honestly tell you that having someone hold me accountable is one of the best gifts I've ever received.

I mean, it sucks sometimes, and I don't enjoy it. But I enjoy *having done* whatever I've been held accountable to. If nothing else, it briefly stops me from hyperfocusing on my internal world.

My Supporter friend asked: "How do we help hold you accountable without feeling like we're parenting you?" I asked my partner, and he said, "I'm not parenting you. I'm holding you accountable as an equal partner and bringing you back to the reality of the situation." I loved that answer!

I think we all need to find what works for our relationship and our individual selves. Plus, each day is different. Some days, you may have the energy and patience to hold your loved one accountable. Other days, you may be experiencing your own brand of the Suck and have zero patience for anyone else.

Sometimes, the most loving thing to do is give hugs and TLC. Other times, the most loving thing to do is to say, "I need you to step outside of yourself and help me."

So, listen to your body and your own needs, and I encourage you both to give yourselves and each other grace as you explore and find your own balance point.

"Do you want solution or comfort?"

A simple solution may seem clear to you during a loved one's Brain Storm, since you're on the outside looking in. Sometimes, we volume control folks want help being pulled out of a Brain Storm. But other times, we just want someone to be like: "Damn that Storm seems like a doozy and I'm going to hang with you until it passes."

Something a friend says to his wife is: "Do you want to be held, heard, or helped?"

Overall, hearing a "this or that" question is much easier for me to handle than an open-ended question. "What can I do to help?" is an open-ended question that makes my brain lock up like an overloaded computer. But something like, "What sounds more helpful, X or Y?" *That*, I can handle. As a friend of mine puts it: "Give me something I can just point at!"

Here's what's great about asking if the Sensitive loved one wants solution or comfort. If they choose *solution*, they're more likely to be receptive to the idea you may have already had! Because now it's *their* idea to hear your idea. This helps the interaction become a true reciprocal conversation rather than you talking *at* them.

As humans, I think we're pretty familiar with what an offering of solution looks like. It's sharing advice, feedback, or a perspective shift. So, *what does offering comfort look like?* The most successful phrase I've experienced is: "I'm sorry. That sucks." Or, "That sounds awful." My partner sometimes goes: "Come here and give me a hug." While I rolled my eyes during the first, say, fifty hugs, I now really love and appreciate the affection.

My partner will often remind me that our relationship is still wonderful, our life is still wonderful: "Nothing has changed between a week ago when you were feeling good about yourself, to now. Only your perspective has changed."

There's about a 50% success rate with that approach. The other half of the time, I flail my arms and stomp away. *Hey, you win some, you lose some.*

So, maybe it's a deep hug and a smooch on the head. Maybe it's a favorite cup of tea or dark chocolate. Or lots of silly GIFs, a handwritten note, or a reminder that you love them even when they're struggling. There's bound to be a bit of trial and error, but I have faith that you'll find what works.

Lovingly boss them around.

If someone asks me what I need or want when I'm in the Suck, the response is typically:

In the last couple of years, my partner has started lovingly bossing me into doing self-care things. Examples: "Stand up. Let's go. We're going to get fresh air on the front porch. Let's go. Up up up up up!" Or, "You need to paint. You've been talking about it for months and haven't done it. Just do one stroke on a canvas." I'll grunt and *HARUMPH* and whine, and then normally do the thing he recommends. And nearly every time, I feel like I can breathe a little easier afterward, like the volume knob has moved down a few ticks.

Note that it's taken us many years to build up to these levels of trust and receptivity. There was way more of a push and pull at first. He thought that when I was on the Struggle Bus, it meant I was unhappy in our relationship and was about to leave him and the kids. I thought that when he offered unsolicited help, it meant he was trying to change me and didn't want to be with someone as "fucked up" as I was. So we'd pull away from each other, when what we really needed to do was *lean in* and open up. There have been many real-talk conversations to get to the level of understanding that we now have.

Plus, there are various spice levels of personality. Some people are more passive or receptive, while others may tend toward being fiery or defensive. Bossing Billy around may work great, but Susan may shut down when being lovingly bossed around. Everyone is different, and every day is different! So, y'know, stay curious to find what works for you and your loved one.

"I still like you."

I think all Earth humans are under a tremendous amount of pressure to be well-behaved and put-together, and we each may feel a little less lovable when we're off our A-game. I tend toward perfectionism, and need help giving myself grace to be in a messy place. I think maybe we all need that same grace.

When a gnarly Storm cloud comes to visit my mind and feelings, I shift into the "reality" (the limiting narrative) that *I'm annoying, a burden, unattractive, unlovable,* and the list goes on. In that state, I'll feel like I always have been and always will be depressed, and I should just save everyone from me.

Getting reassurance from my partner and my friends while I'm in the Suck and *especially* once I'm out of it? Oh, it's balm to my weary soul. I mean, sometimes I'm *not* the most receptive to reassurance, but I'm working on it. My partner used to say: "Just so you know, I still love you." And I'd be like:

So now he says, "I still love *and like* you, even when you're struggling." With my closest friends, we know each other well enough to even ask for reassurance. "Can you please tell me it's okay for me to feel like a shitshow disaster right now?"

It's important to self-soothe and say these loving things to ourselves. But community is also important! They[60] say it takes a village. Maybe your loved one needs a reminder that they're still a delight, even when in the Suck. And you can even ask them for a reminder that *they* still like *you*, even when they're struggling.

Clear is kind.

Being a highly sensitive person, I've always had a sense of underlying truth. Even as a kid, I could tell when there was unspoken tension between people. (Unfortunately, I then took it upon myself to resolve the issue for both people, which I wasn't even remotely equipped to do.)

So, if someone says one thing but my intuition says another, I feel properly crazy. Rigorous honesty has become the most important thing to me in any relationship (including my relationship with myself). Rigorous honesty is one of the key principles of recovery, and it's changed my life. I don't just mean simply telling the truth; I'm talking about *a deep commitment to authenticity, no matter how uncomfortable or difficult that may be.*

Yes, someone being super direct can hurt my feelings. But, once I breathe through the discomfort and my

---

[60] Who is "they"? I mean, someone had to be the very first person to say a saying, right?! *does a trust fall down the rabbit hole*

nervous system settles, I'm really grateful that the person cut through the noise with honesty. And over time, with practice (and space to recover my tender, bruised feelings), accepting feedback no longer hijacks my nervous system! My world has gotten bigger, because I'm no longer afraid of people being *real* with me.

Being in a relationship with a volume control loved one can feel like you're orbiting around them. For years (decades, even) I acted like the world revolved around me and expected everyone to avoid hurting my feelings. Turns out, that was unfair to them and to myself. Everyone felt on edge around me and, meanwhile, my expectation of them to kid-glove my feelings meant I was stopping myself from learning how to, well, *fully engage with life.*

What I'm saying is: **It's important to express your opinions and feelings.** Just because your Sensitive loved one may have intense emotional reactions at times doesn't mean you should suppress your own emotions and thoughts. That's unfair to you, because then you're carrying around the building tension of words left unsaid. It's unfair to them because they don't know that you're struggling or have something you really need to say. Resentment poisons relationships.

I have personally found that being *clear and direct* is better than trying to add a bunch of fluff to soften the blow. By "fluff" I mean when we add a bunch of softening language on top of our message because we're so afraid to hurt someone's feelings. Plot twist: When we add fluff on top of our actual message, that leaves more room for misinterpretation!

If you're not sure what "clear and direct" looks like, here's an idea. Think of something you really want to say to your loved one. (You know the thing. It just popped in your head.) You can even write it down, if that's your jam. Answer the following questions:

1. How could you say this to them in a way that *avoids hurting their feelings*? (So fluffy.)

2. If you had complete freedom to speak your mind *without worrying about their feelings*, what would you say? (Zero fluff.)

Now, compare the two.

There isn't one that's right or wrong. Rather, I encourage you to remove a bit of the fluff to get closer to what you're really trying to say. Or, if you're someone who is *so* direct that you've been called *a bit harsh*, you can instead use this exercise to explore how to add a wee bit of cushion. (My preference is zero fluff. Get right to it!)

In my experience, this rigorously honest approach takes practice, but it's worth it. It cuts through the bullshit and saves a lot of time and heartache.

Either way, your loved one's reaction could very likely be LOUD. So why not say exactly what you need to say?

Then, once they settle down, you can have a conversation from a calm place with less bottled-up resentment.

To help *you* help *them* help *you*

Learn what's helpful and unhelpful to say.

Here are examples of real-life things said to me when I've been in the Suck:

"You have so much to be grateful for. You should make a gratitude list!" – "There are people who have to walk miles and miles just to get water. Your life is great in comparison." – "Just think happy thoughts."

For me, **these are entirely unhelpful**. Why?

- **(Re: gratitude)** – I logically know that I have so much to be grateful for. And yet, I feel lousy and miserable. This disconnect only adds to the Suck.
- **(Re: others have it worse)** – Yes, there are people who have it much worse than me. The very fact that anyone is suffering anywhere is something that's on my mind pretty much constantly. As such, a reminder that others are suffering in no way stops my own pain. It's all relative.
- **(Re: happy thoughts)** – Telling a depressed person to think positively is like telling someone with a sour

lemon stuck in their mouth to "just think about sweet things." Or if you were super sensitive to spice and someone was like, "Oh, come on! It's not that spicy!" while you have spice-induced snot and tears spewing from your face holes. For you, it *is* spicy!

Over the last few years, I've really focused on learning what feels good, on what feels helpful. There are certain phrases that cut through all the emotional noise and get right to my very core.

I'll share the phrases – those cheat codes – that typically work for me, and maybe you and your Sensitive loved one can practice and experiment with these and others. Please only use phrases that feel honest to you.

Helpful things to say to me during a Brain Storm:

"BE gENtlE with yourself.

You got this."

"SOME AMAZiNg NUggEt of wisdom is comiNg fRom this paiN.

DoN't give up."

"I'll hold doWN the foRt while you'RE stRuggliNg."

The goal isn't to feel like you're walking a tightrope, forced to bite your tongue. Rather, the goal is to offer encouragement and love *in the way your loved one receives encouragement and love.* And in a way that you feel comfortable offering it.

Perhaps we can think of the list of helpful phrases as "cheat codes." Dare to be curious and experiment to learn what your loved one's cheat codes are and are not. Yes, sometimes you'll get it wrong. But when you get it right? It's a powerful moment when, even in the midst of a Brain Storm, you catch a glimmer of recognition and receptivity in your loved one's eyes.

Discuss what a true crisis looks like.

My lifelong Supporter friend, Tyler, shared with me: "We [as Supporters] are afraid because we cannot resonate with your thoughts of suicide or deep, dark times. We don't know what a *true crisis* looks like when y'all's everyday-dark-day looks *pretty fucking scary* to us."

Hopefully, the code words (page 210) can help you begin to learn what is and isn't a **RED ALERT** situation. From there, the knowledge comes from *experience* and learning about your individual loved one (and them learning about you).

And ideally, the "true crisis" insights are discussed during a grounded time where a loved one *isn't* in a crisis.

But if they *are* in the Suck right now and you're unsure what to do, maybe take note of their behaviors or what they're saying. Hold onto this information for when they're out of the Suck. From there, you can start a conversation of: "Here's what I noticed. What did you mean by that? Can you help me better understand?"

Everyone's crisis looks different. Some people may be explosive. Others may become super internal and hide from the world. Every person has their own personality, needs, and way of handling (or hiding from) emotions. Life is an ongoing journey of learning from one another. Over time, after surviving Brain Storms together and having reflective discussions afterward, you and your loved one will have a much clearer idea of what *is* and is *not* a crisis.

This is especially important for Supporters, because trying to decipher what is or isn't a crisis becomes extremely taxing over time. You adore your volume control loved one, so it makes sense that you want to do everything you can to help them. But **you can't be their hero**. That's unfair to you and to them and isn't sustainable.

Supporter burnout is a real thing. Let's work together to avoid it. Any flavor of relationship is a two-way street, and hopefully some of *Volume Control*'s tips and tricks can help you balance the scales.

And if you are ever truly concerned for your or their lives, please seek professional help[61]. I've also added my favorite resources at the end of the book to further help you on your Supporter journey.

Thank you for your willingness to be on this journey.

Ask questions after the Suck passes.

When the volume knobs balance out after your loved one's Brain Storm passes, that's an opportunity to get curious and start a conversation. Discuss what the Ouch was about (if they know), what the experience was like, or

---

[61] To get help supporting a loved one in crisis, text or call 988 (U.S. only), or visit https://988lifeline.org/chat/

what they may have needed that they didn't get. (Please also share what *you* needed that you didn't get.)

Keep that information tucked away in your mind palace (or on the notebook pages at the end of this section) and reference those notes during the next Brain Storm. The notes are like a study guide. By having the study guide handy, the next tough situation can be more like an open-book test and less like an unexpected pop quiz.

This Storm-free time is also an ideal opportunity to come up with the code word or phrase (page 210), and a plan for what actions to take when the phrase is used.

Keep in mind: This conversation isn't intended to be a *you* versus *them* thing. **You're on the same team.** You may need to remind them of that, or even remind yourself. How can we figure this out *together?*

And if they get super pissy about your attempts at a conversation or feel like you're trying to *fix them*, maybe try a comparison such as: "If I regularly got an upset stomach or gnarly headaches, wouldn't you want to work together to find the best way to help me?"

This is not a fixing situation. This is a *translation* situation. They experience life one way, and you another. You're learning to bridge the communication gap. It's hard work, and it is so very worth it. *You* are so very worth it.

DIY (how to make your own)

Hopefully, you can use some of what you've read in *Volume Control* as a starting point for your own reference book. We are completely different humanoids, so I expect that there are parts of *Volume Control* that didn't quite resonate with you. Or maybe some of my tricks reminded you of something slightly different that works better for you. *Excellent.* I included notebook paper at the end of each section as a note-taking spot for your ideas as you're reading. **Yes! It's okay to write in the book.** This book is meant to be used and personalized. So, write in the margins and highlight passages. Or keep it pristine and put your notes elsewhere, if that's your thing.

So, how do you open a line of communication between your Stormy Self and Sunny Self?

I'm going to say the thing that I hate hearing: *There's no right or wrong way to do this.* I must remind myself of this fact often because I, erm, *happen to be a wee bit of a perfectionist.* I lived much of my life with the belief: "If I can't do it perfectly, I shan't do it at all!" And then I sulked as I watched life pass me by.

Obviously, the self-awareness journey is a messy, at-times ugly one. Doing it perfectly would remove the humanness of our experience. In this case (and in most cases), *done is better than perfect.* Any action step, no matter how wobbly, is better than taking zero action and sitting in the Suck forever. Scribbling some messy nonsense through snot and tears is better than holding it all in and imploding.

I remember the exact day I first wrote down what I was emotionally experiencing, while I was experiencing it. I was in my late twenties, still wrestling a slew of addictions, and still very much held captive by suicidality. I'd get super triggered out of nowhere, spiral into a deep darkness, drink a handle of vodka, chew pain pills, eat a bunch of processed junk food, and ultimately want to kill myself because the pain seemed to last forever.

See – the addictions worked, *until they didn't.* I had held in my emotions for so long that, no matter what I ingested or did, it no longer touched the pain. The emotions were too loud and desperate for my attention.

There I was, in my 575-square-foot apartment near Kennesaw State University, caught in the grip of another suicidal panic attack. And those really deep, dark episodes seem to last *forever* when I'm in them.

But then, out of nowhere, a tiny sliver of curiosity plopped into my mind grapes: *This may feel like forever, but I wonder how long these episodes actually last?*

I sat at my IKEA kitchen table and cracked open a blank journal. I wrote down the time the emotional spinout started and what I was feeling. I recalled what had most recently happened right before the spiral. I wrote down what I was craving, how much alcohol and which foods I consumed, and ultimately when the episode ended.

The suicidal episode that felt like it was lasting forever? It ended up being 30 minutes! I'm 97% certain and 4% bad math that 30 minutes is *less than forever*. What a relief!

That was my very first *AHA!* moment, my first glimpse into what it was like to *witness* my experience rather than be held captive by it. I continued to journal in this way for months.

I learned that my episodes were rarely, if ever, out of nowhere. They often had a clear pattern and a clear trigger. I also learned that my deeply suicidal episodes lasted, on average, for 15-30 minutes. An hour tops. This knowledge left me feeling hopeful for the first time ever. As all-encompassing as the depressive panicky times felt, I learned *through my own experience* that they'd soon run their course. I had real-life data to back up this claim.

From there, I started employing a few healthier coping skills when spinning out, and wrote down how they worked. When a suicidal episode started, I'd stare at the damn clock, clutch the table, and do my best to shakily breathe my way through it. I'd remind myself: "30 minutes. I only have to make it another 30 minutes. I can do *anything* for 30 minutes."

I became my own little research project. Rather than feel helpless and out of control, I was starting to learn the language of my emotions and my body. And learn what they were trying to say to me.

Perhaps you can start a journal or a cheat sheet much like the one you're reading right now. Or get wild with it, snag some colorful pens, and write directly in this book. Your notes may seem scattered at first. That's okay. Over time, as you revisit and add more insights, I'm confident you'll find themes and organize the information in a way that best benefits your brain.

Here's how I envision *Volume Control* being used:

First time reading...

Read the book from beginning to end[62].

Next handful of readthroughs...

When you're in the *1-5's (or 0)*

Read the corresponding section and *write to your sunnier, Future Self.* (See **Approach 1: The two-way radio** on the next page.)

When you're in the *6-10's (or 11)*

Read the corresponding section and *read and respond to what your past Stormy Self wrote.* This is an opportunity to pay it forward to Future You. (If you couldn't articulate

---

[62] Can you think of others who'd love this book? Tell them about it!

your feelings during the **1-5's**, check out **Approach 2: The hindsight insight** on page 327.)

From then on...

Once you've moved through the above cycle a few times: Simply choose your own adventure (and section) based on your emotional state! Pay special attention to the tips and tricks you've compiled for yourself.

Next up, I've shared some examples of what works for me when opening a line of communication between Stormy Jen and Sunny Jen. Please be kind to yourself and recognize that this isn't remotely an overnight task. Take your time, and try to stay curious and even playful as you explore what works for you.

Approach 1: The two-way radio

This is where the real magic happens: when we dare to express what we're experiencing *during* the Suck, the Brain Storm, the Quicksand, the depressive episode. It is time to wield the pen while we've got the fuck-its or feel like the world is caving in on us. **We are writing to our Future Self**, opening a conversation. When the clouds lift, *Sunnier You* can respond.

A few questions when writing from an activated place may be:

- **What emotional state are you in?** (Use my 1-10 "radio channels" or whatever works for you.)
- **What does it feel like?** (What are the physical sensations in your body? What thoughts are rolling around in your noggin?)
- **What do you need?** (Or what do you not need?)

This mindset is one of the hardest places to share from, especially at first. As I mentioned earlier in the book, when I first started tuning into my emotions, everything felt like "AAAHHHH!" As such, my first entries when in an activated mindset were like: "I don't know what the fuck I'm feeling I just know it sucks and I want a burger."

Here's a good follow-up question if your ouchy mindset writing is initially vague or a big mess of brain barf: **"Why?"**

I don't know what the fuck I'm feeling I just know it sucks and I want a burger.

Why?

Because I'm hungry and want something that's greasy.

Why?

Fuck you, why. Because I eat healthily all the goddamn time and I'm tired of trying to be so perfect.

Thank you for this information.

Now Future Jen has something to work with! When the clouds lift and I feel less activated, I go back and read what I wrote during the Suck. Let's use the above example of, "I don't know *what the fuck* I'm feeling." I'd categorize this as a **3-4** mindset. While everything felt messy and irritating during the **3-4**, I can now see clear themes: *perfectionism, trying too hard, needing a break, wanting a treat, feeling like I need permission for a break or treat.* Sunnier Jen's note back could be something like:

HEY, JEN at a 4.

I hEREby give you pERMissioN to
EAt a buRgER, watch shows, &
cANcEl plANs. You woRk hARd.
You dESERve to give youRsElf a
bREAk!

LOVE, JEN at AN 8

The next time I'm at a **3** or **4**, I go back and review the ongoing conversation between Past Jens. I have evidence (in writing!) that I've been in this headspace before, and it will eventually lift. Also, I have guidance from Jen at an **8** who clearly sees the themes I'm struggling with. Maybe I'll implement her advice and then add a follow-up note about the results.

Approach 2: The hindsight insight

I shared the first example of this approach in section **6** on page 196. Hindsight is a delightful frenemy of mine on this road trip of life. Normally, when the Brain Storm clouds lift from my mind and I can hear the birds chirping again[63], I'll get a wave of clarity of what the emotional Storm was all about. I'll look back over the previous days or weeks and have a new depth of understanding about what was happening, how I felt, and what I needed.

The hindsight approach is a way to retroactively give a voice to the voiceless part of ourselves. This way, we can learn from the experience and pay it forward to Future Us who may similarly struggle. We're compassionately researching and exploring our behaviors, writing them down, and learning from our experience.

A few questions when writing hindsight insight may be:

- **What is clear to me now that wasn't during the Brain Storm?**
- **What did I need?**
- **What emotional state was I in? What was I feeling?**
- **What can I do differently next time to better fulfill my needs?**
- **What action step can I take right now (to make amends or prepare for future Brain Storms)?**

---

[63] Likely bragging about their barf, which is totally understandable.

Hindsight insight example 2

Hindsight insight: When I said I was fine, I really meant I wasn't fine and needed help. I just didn't know how to explain that, and I was too afraid to seem needy or like a burden. This mostly frustrated me and my partner because we both just wanted to be close to each other but were afraid to do the wrong thing. It was like walking on eggshells and it sucked.

What I needed: I don't really know what I needed, honestly. I sort of wanted to lay face first on the floor and scream. Maybe that's what I needed? Also, watching Mrs. Doubtfire sounds fun. Is that weird? Maybe it is weird. Maybe it's okay to be weird.

What emotional state I was in: I think this was a 2. I wasn't to the point of giving up on life, but I felt damn close.

What to do next time: Next time, I'll be more honest about how I feel rather than saying "fine." I'll focus more on helping myself and others through honesty rather than trying to save them from me.

Action step to take now: I'll make amends with my partner. I'll let them know I was nervous to upset them or burden them. I'll share more about what the Brain Storm was like for me, what I was thinking and feeling, and also give them space to share their experience.

Maybe the Storm will ultimately help us communicate more clearly overall?

I don't know. Maybe.

The goal of these exercises is to help Future You quickly navigate to the section that holds the help you'll need.

Then, we can add *the two-way radio* or *hindsight insight* information to the appropriate section of your in-progress guidebook. If you're customizing a printed copy of this book, *Volume Control*, I recommend adding a personalized phrase to the table of contents for the emotional state you were recently in. Here's how that may look, using the example from *the two-way radio* approach on page 326.

Emotional state	Description
4 SOMETHING'S NOT RIGHT	**Read when:** • Thoughts are spinning. • You feel uncomfortable, like your skin doesn't fit. • It feels impossible to get up and get going. • You can't tell what's real. *(Add your own.)* • I can't tell WHAT I'm feeling. •

These are two approaches that have worked for me. But, again, there's no right or wrong way to do this. You can use notebook paper, the margins of this book, a text document, or a note-taking app in your phone. Let it be messy. **Something is better than nothing**, and this won't be an overnight experience. It took me over five years to compile this book, *and I'm a professional writer!*

Give yourself some grace, patience, and permission to laugh at the stumbles along the way.

When to share your findings.

In the early stages of dating my partner, he'd get overwhelmed by novel-length text messages from me at 2AM explaining that I'd just had a deep emotional release and here's all the old stories that came up and here is what I learned from it and *and* **and**.

He's a dad with two kids and a full-time job where he does something important that I don't understand. He doesn't have time to be my diary, nor is he particularly interested in a deep analytical rundown of every hiccup in life. Most people don't have as deep of an interest in inner workings and behind-the-scenes analysis as I do. I have one special friend (hi, Sandy!) who I know I can word vomit to, free of judgment. And she does the same to me. We spew all our exciting self-realizations at one another, and we love every second of it and celebrate with many, many GIFs. But this isn't sustainable in every relationship.

Apparently, people have entire lives outside of me and my emotions. *Gasp!*

So, I don't have to explain myself all the time. I don't have to share every miniscule detail of what's going on with me. I'm not the star of a reality show with people awaiting an update after every crying spell or bout of gas. Yes, it is important to share. It's also important to stay mindful of other people, their needs, and to ask them what's going on in *their* world. Know your audience.

Obviously, I'm not as picky about my audience's needs when I'm in a **1-4** headspace. I know it's far more important for me to share and reach out for help when I'm struggling than it is to try and deduce whether someone else is in the space to receive me. I leave that for **6+** mindsets.

I used to talk with (at?) people, waiting for them to take a tiny inhalation so I could sneak in and share my hour-long story about my past life and how it shows up in this lifetime and what that means for future relationship dynamics. Meanwhile, they're like:

So yes, I encourage a lot of sharing throughout this book. As you get more comfortable doing so, I also encourage you to be mindful of your audience! They're humans with feelings and an entire life, too. No matter how much a Supporter or friend adores you, they will never care as much as you do about your experience and realizations, because they have their own experience and realizations to focus on.

It's like when a person tries to tell you about a wild dream they had that they think is so cool and meaningful. Meanwhile, you're eager for the weird-ass dream recall to end because the storyline is all over the place and impossible to follow.

I imagine that's how I come across when I share my in-depth emotional analysis with my partner at 11:30PM on a school night.

No matter how well we describe what we experience, there is no way another person will *fully* understand it, especially if they're a Supporter and not a Sensitive. (This is also why I love therapy because I can spew all the inner workings of my mind to someone who *must sit and listen.* Plus, she is *also* a brain nerd who's dedicated to understanding behavior. It's glorious.)

People either experience life like we do, or they don't. Occasionally, folks will have situational depressive episodes and go: "Oh wow, is this what it's like for you all the time? This sucks!"

A friend called me one night in a panic. She'd always been the grounded one, the stable one. This night, she was experiencing suicidality for the first time in her life.

"I have no idea how you've lived with this as long as you have," she said to me through tears. "It is terrifying. I feel like I can't trust myself or my thoughts and that is so scary. And this is *one night.* You've dealt with this for most of your life. Holy shit, you're strong."

I hated that she was in pain but became grateful that she was getting an insider's view. It felt good to know how to show up for her. It also felt good to be understood.

But guess what? That won't always be the case. Not everyone experiences life the way we do. My partner and sponsor, for instance, have no idea what it's like to deal with suicidality. They can't even fathom it.

Meanwhile, when they go on about how they experience daily life, I'm like:

You mean not everyone has to convince themselves to stay alive each day?

It's important to share. It's imperative to keep loved ones in the loop, especially if we're in a true crisis or early in our recovery journey. But if they don't respond with the excitement or dramatic gasp you think they should? Let it go. Their view of life is far different from yours. You're a supporting actor to their life story. *No one will care about this as much as you*, and that's okay.

If you really want to share about your breakthroughs and your Supporters are unavailable, consider journaling or writing a blog entry. Ooo, and therapy! My friend says that finding a good therapist is like finding a good bra. *We feel supported but free enough to be ourselves.*

I'm also learning it's okay to sometimes keep my realizations warm and cozy to myself. Not to *hide* them, but to have a sense of intimacy with myself. I am still discovering what that balance is, especially as someone who shares my behind-the-scenes so publicly.

I lived at one extreme for a while – holding everything in until I imploded. Then, I swung to the other end of the pendulum and shared every thought, feeling, and sneeze with the world. Now, I'm settling somewhere in the middle.

I'm confident that you'll find your balance point, too.

Thanks for stopping by (closing thoughts)

Everyone handles their sensitivities differently. Some numb through drinking and drugs. Others gobble sugary items, binge-watch Netflix, or get sucked into social media. Some even overindulge on self-help, finding a seemingly healthy expression for an inner desire to control, fix, and hide from whatever sucks ass *right now*. There also may be a mystical few who handle it all well. I've yet to meet them, but they may exist. They probably have great hair.

My personal numb-of-choice was suicidality — this obsessive/possessive thought that, no matter what, I could always check out and leave. Like an emergency escape route, or a self-destruct button.

Whatever our *way out* is or was, the fact remains the same: **Some of us have the volume turned way up on life.** What does this mean? It means we experience emotions more deeply, and typical aspects of being human can feel extra challenging due to how loud and spiky life can be.

Great news: It's not the end of the world. It's not a curse. *It doesn't have to be debilitating.*

I used to interpret the phrase "You're so sensitive" as an insult.

Now I list it as one of my favorite assets.

When I say "sensitive," I don't just mean someone who gets their feelings easily hurt. I'm referring to something deeper. Energetic sensitivity. Spiritual sensitivity. Emotional, mental, and physical sensitivities, too. There are different words I could use, like empath or intuitive, but those still don't fully encompass it.

As I said at the beginning of this book: If you are a person with the volume turned up, you likely know it. Maybe not in those exact words, but you know you're different in *some* way. And now? I hope you see that **you're not alone**.

I do not know your individual battle. I do not know which diagnoses, if any, you've been labeled with. I do not know the pain you feel or the demons you fight. I don't know your past, your personal sensitivities, the traumas you've endured, or what your triggers may be.

But I do know mine. And if someone who has attempted suicide, seen demons, suffered from addiction and disordered eating, been hospitalized and heavily medicated, and who had to fight herself to stay alive for two decades... is now able to hold down a big kid job, have healthy relationships, wake up feeling grateful at best and *okay* at worst, finally keep plants alive[64], and do all of it in sobriety? *waves* I can confidently say *you've got a chance, too.*

---

[64] Okay, *some* plants.

Wanting to die is what ultimately taught me how to live.

Retraining and healing takes time and effort. And rest and nurturing and naps and floor cries. I've found it to be an ongoing balancing act of nurturing myself *and* pushing myself. Each of us must find that balance for ourselves. This work isn't for the faint of heart. It is hard work to learn to rewrite our perception of life, to adjust our reactions and responses. And it's totally worth it. *You're worth it.*

I ended the book with a cheesy comment. *I love cheese.*

I hope this nifty little book of cheat codes and course corrections has been helpful for you, and I hope you keep it handy for future reference to help you with your volume control. And please gift or recommend it to friends who may also benefit from it. This book's reach is entirely word of mouth and synchronicity. *Thank you for your support.*

And remember: No matter what happens? **Stay.**

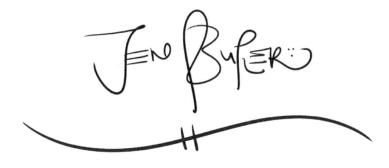

Jen who? (about the author)

Jen Butler (@jenbutlersays) is a writer, comedian, and content creator in recovery from alcoholism, addiction, self-harm, suicidality, disordered eating, codependency, BII (Breast Implant Illness), cancer, and an odd period when she only listened to dubstep.

Jen's goals are to help complex or taboo issues (such as suicidality, depression, and overall mental health) become more digestible through her vulnerable, comedic approach.

In addition to creative non-fiction, Jen also writes feature-length dark comedy screenplays. Through her writing and videos, she hopes to help people feel less alone in their messy humanness, and to bridge the communication gap between those who experience life with the volume turned way up and those who don't.

When not getting lost in creative expression, you can find Jen training in martial arts, taking an improv class, watching The Matrix for the literal 500th time, or enjoying a delightful, long nap.

She lives in Georgia with her partner, two bonus kiddos, three dogs, and one cat with a gloriously fluffy tail.

@jenbutlersays
www.jenbutlersays.com

Jen's favorite resources!

Books

- **"Alcoholics Anonymous: The Big Book"** by Anonymous. Alcoholics Anonymous World Services, Inc., 2002. — *(Working the 12 steps has been a spiritual experience. I live a rigorously honest life and no longer carry around resentment or shame.)*
- **"The Artist's Way: 30th Anniversary Edition"** by Julia Cameron. TarcherPerigee, 2016. — *(Amazing inner child work.)*
- **"The Big Leap: Conquer Your Hidden Fear and Take Life to the Next Level"** by Gay Hendricks. EFINITO, 2010. — *(Continues to help me expand in love, abundance, and success every day as I inspire those around me to do the same.)*
- **"Codependent No More: How to Stop Controlling Others and Start Caring for Yourself"** by Melody Beattie. Spiegel & Grau, 2022. — *(An essential read for caregivers who focus too much on others. Especially helpful for any +1 Supporters.)*
- **"Depressive Illness: The Curse of the Strong"** by Dr. Tim Cantopher. Sheldon Press, 2012. — *(This book taught me compassion for my experience with depression.)*
- **"The Empath's Survival Guide: Life Strategies for Sensitive People"** by Judith Orloff. Sounds True Adult, 2018. — *(Tips to take care of one's own energy.)*
- **"The End of Your World: Uncensored Straight Talk on the Nature of Enlightenment"** by Adyashanti. Sounds True, 2009. — *(Reading this helped me understand why a spiritual awakening can feel awfully similar to schizophrenia.)*
- **"The Four Agreements: A Practical Guide to Personal Freedom (A Toltec Wisdom Book)"** by Don Miguel Ruiz. Amber-Allen Publishing, Incorporated, 1997. — *(A short, simple, and profound book that everyone in the world should read.)*
- **"Loving What Is, Revised Edition: Four Questions That Can Change Your Life; The Revolutionary Process Called 'The Work'"** by Byron Katie, Stephen Mitchell. Harmony, 2021. — *(If you're ready to take responsibility for your behavior, buy this book. The Judge Your Neighbor worksheet is amazing.)*
- **"Present Perfect: A Mindfulness Approach to Letting Go of Perfectionism and the Need for Control"** by Pavel G

Somov PhD. New Harbinger Publications, 2010. — *(Helped me curb perfectionistic compulsions that plagued me for decades.)*
- **"The Untethered Soul: The Journey Beyond Yourself"** by Michael A. Singer. New Harbinger Publications/Noetic Books, 2007. — *(This is literally my most favorite book ever in all the land. If you're ready to extend beyond your "limits," give it a try.)*

Apps

- **Clue period tracker**. — *(To keep track of my cycles.)*
- **Finch: Self Care Pet**. — *(Cute-ifies self-care. Adorable. Try it.)*
- **Insight Timer**. — *(Free meditation app. Check out my meditations! @jenbutlersays)*

Products and other goodies

- **Inner balance**. store.heartmath.com/innerbalance — *(It's a cool ear clippy thing with an app that teaches you how to **breathe** in an equal and balanced way.)*
- **Shakti mat**. shaktimat.com — *(This acupressure mat resets my nervous system and calms me down. Not for the faint of heart.)*
- **Vipassana meditation retreat**. dhamma.org — *(Doing a 10-day silent meditation retreat was one of the most challenging, profound experiences of my life.)*

International emergency service websites

- **Befrienders Worldwide.** befrienders.org – Displays closest crisis centers and contact information based on your location.
- **IASP (International Association of Suicide Prevention).** findahelpline.com – Free, confidential support via online chat, text, or phone.

Specialized resources (abuse and assault hotline, LGBTQIA+) here: https://www.cdc.gov/mentalhealth/tools-resources/index.htm

Acknowledge-mints

Special thanks to my beta readers: Adonia, Bethany, Brittany, Elana, Katrina, Kevin, Lauren, Lindsey, Meghan, Minne, and Vernessa. To Ale and Tyler, who jumped in to help at the last minute with such care and presence. A cyber squeeze to my cover designer and friend, Andrea, for guiding me through 50+ iterations and as many existential crises. A GIF-inspired hug to my assistant and sanity-saver, Lauren. Big sourdough love to my "soup mate," Jess, for continuing to remind me of what's important. Thank you for your ongoing battle with Matt re: Neil Young. It's the gift that keeps on giving.

Thank you to Sandy and Hailey for keeping me on Earth during the hardest years of my life, and for loving me no matter how stinky or depressed or hyper. Oh, and Sandy? Thanks for that time you pretended to be my mom to get me out of work when I was having back-to-back panic attacks. You are my *lifer* best friend.

Olivia: my idea incubator, improv queen, and forever cheerleader. How did we get so lucky to find each other?

Mommy, Dad (aka Poops), and Chipper: Thank you for believing in me, supporting me through the highs and lows, and for cooking me delicious meals. That last part is mostly for Chip. You're a genius chef.

To Matt, my best friend and toe tether: I forever appreciate your ongoing support of my 9,002 endeavors, while also reminding me to do human things such as eat and rest. I love you for your rigorous honesty and ongoing willingness to build a balanced, supportive, and hilarious partnership. And thank you and Jem for making two of the raddest kids ever and inviting me into your life to help raise them.

And to my online supporters: I am regularly humbled and validated by your love and encouragement. I am you and you are me and we are SPARTA! Wait, no. Just... thank you. If we're gonna be on this Earth human study abroad trip, I'm glad we're here together.

Printed in the USA
CPSIA information can be obtained
at www.ICGtesting.com
LVHW021613011124
795435LV00040B/762